50 BEST
PUB
CRAWLS
in England, Scotland, Wales & Ireland

BARRIE PEPPER • DAVID PERROT

CAMRA BOOKS

STOREY BOOKS

The mission of Storey Communications is to serve our customers by publishing practical information that encourages personal independence in harmony with the environment.

North American edition published in 2000 by Storey Books, Schoolhouse Road, Pownal, Vermont 05261.

United Kingdom edition published in 2000 by CAMRA Books, Campaign for Real Ale, 230 Hatfield Road, St. Albans AL1 4LW.

Edited by Mark Webb (CAMRA), Jeanée Ledoux, and Brad Ring (Storey Books)
Cover and text design and production by McKie Associates
Cover photographs by Tracey Sherwood
Maps by Perrott Cartographics
Indexed by Linda and David Buskus, Northwind Editorial Services

Printed in the United States by Versa Press
10 9 8 7 6 5 4 3 2 1

Library of Congress Cataloging-in-Publication Data

Pepper, Barrie.
    50 best pub crawls in England, Scotland, Wales and Ireland / Barrie
Pepper, David Perrot.
      p.   cm.
    ISBN 1-58017-177-X (alk. paper)
    1. Bars (Drinking establishments)-Great Britain. I. Title: Fifty best pub
crawls in England, Scotland, Wales and Ireland. II. Perrot, David. III. Title.
TX950.59.G7 P47 2000
647.95'0941-dc21   99-050081

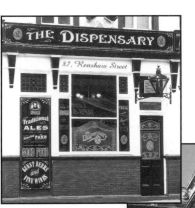

CONTENTS

INTRODUCTION

Pub crawling in England, Scotland, Wales and Ireland has been an activity for as long as we have had pubs. The stages of stage-coaching were pubs, and a journey from, say, Leeds to London in the 18th century would take three days from start to finish with two overnight stops and a number of refreshment stops at inns, pubs, and taverns.

These were the first long-distance pub crawls. Later, from the industrial revolution onwards, workers would regulate their homeward journey after a hard-worked shift by stops at pubs. An uncle of mine, a miner, told me how on payday he would visit up to eight pubs on his way home from the pit. Knowing him, and my aunt, he would not have another drink for a week.

Many towns, particularly northern industrial ones, have what is known in many places as a "stagger," which these days takes on the more dignified title of "circuit drinking." These are simply visits to a continual series of pubs without missing any, often along one road. It probably means visiting some good pubs, some bad pubs, and some indistinctive ones. The fine art of pub crawl-ing is to work out a route that allows you to visit a number of pubs, all selling good beers and, ideally, of some character and interest. And even better that the crawl should start and finish close to the same point and near to good public transport con-nections. Of course this is not always possible, but this book attempts to give you a selection that comes close to the ideal. Occasionally you will find pubs marked in bold italics, which means that they are in the "try also" category. If you have time, call in; otherwise, pass on.

Some of these pub crawls are in city centers, while others are sub-urban. Some are in country towns, while one or two are in vil-lages. And then there is a selection of unusual crawls: by train, by boat, by supertram, and a couple of country rambles. Many of the crawls take you to places of interest other than pubs — castles, churches, stately homes, museums, and even breweries. And there is a reasonable geographical spread, although I am conscious of the fact that certain areas are not covered very well. On the other hand, there are some parts of the country where a group of crawls is close enough together to warrant thinking about short holidays and weekends pub crawling. Ideas for new pub crawls for anoth-er edition of this guide are welcome.

It is an irony that within weeks of signing the contract to edit this guide I started to feel the pains of osteoarthritis in my right knee. It is the sort of disease that doesn't get better. And then halfway through the writing I undertook major heart surgery, which was a great success but knocked my work back by six months. Therefore many of these pub crawls will remain either within my memory or will be far from attainment. However, the pleasure of compiling the guide overcomes the albeit painful disadvantage of not being able to use it myself, and I hope it will give you, the reader, much pleasure and entertainment.

Thanks Due

Thanks is due to the following for their help in compiling this guidebook. They were either instrumental in suggesting and outlining a pub crawl, in taking photographs and roughing out maps, or simply being helpful. There will be tangible "thank yous" as well:

Dave Backhouse, Yvette and Neil Bacon, Roy Bailey, Gavin Brammer, Mark Bridges, Rob Buckley, Martin Butler, Andy Camroux, Alan Canvess, John Clarke, Pearl Claydon, the late Ivor Clissold, John Corcoran, Lucie Edginton, Peter Edwardson, Martin Ellis, Brian Glover, Spike Golding, Dave Haddon, Michael Hardman, John Holland, George Howie, Mark Hutchinson, Linda Hutton, Rhys Jones, Sean Kelleher, Jim Lawrie, Richard Lycett, the Northern Ireland Tourist Office, John McCloy, Charles McMaster, Susan and Fran Nowak, Chris Palmer, Ken Paris, Tracey Parker, David Pepper, Tim Proudfoot, Roger Protz, Richard Putley, Jim Scanlon, the Severn Valley Railway Company, Andrew Shrigley, John Simpson, Gordon Small, Geoff Strawbridge, Martin Strawbridge, Chris Stringer, Karl Thomson, Rob Tough, Colin Valentine, Ralph Warrington, Nick Whitaker, John White, Drew Whiteley, Keith Wilson, and Andy Wright.

And to members of the following branches of CAMRA: Abercolwyn, Aberdeen, Grampian and Northern Isles, Arun and Adur, Bridgenorth Sub Branch, Bristol and District, Burton upon Trent and South Derbyshire, Chester and South Clwyd, Derby, Edinburgh and South East Scotland, Exeter and East Devon, Gloucestershire, Herefordshire, High Peak and North East Cheshire, Hull and East Yorkshire, Kidderminster Sub Branch,

Louth, Merseyside, North Sussex, Nottingham, Sheffield, South East London, South West London, Stockport and South Manchester, Sunderland and South Tyneside, Swindon and North Wiltshire, Tyneside and Northumberland, Walsall, West Lancashire, and York.

Also to Mark Webb, who kept me on the straight and narrow; David Perrott, who drew some superb maps; and Phillip Tordoff, Howard Bicknell, and Jack Thompson, who gave help that went far beyond the call of duty. I owe them all a few pints. And finally, I must single out for special mention my dear wife Carolynne for all her help, kindness, and encouragement during the protracted preparations for this book. As usual, she was prepared to drive me to the pub. And back again.

Barrie Pepper

BARRIE PEPPER is one of England's best known beer writers. He has recently retired as Chairman of the British Guild of Beer Writers after seven years in office. This is his 14th book, and his previous ones include *Irish Pubs, The International Book of Beer, The Bedside Book of Beer,* and *The Old Inns and Pubs of Leeds.* He writes for *What's Brewing, Pub Management Magazine, American Brewer,* the *Yorkshire Post,* and several other newspapers and journals. His other interests include sport and music, and he enjoys good company and conversation in the convivial atmosphere of genuine pubs. He and his wife, Carolynne, who runs a beer shop, live in one of the leafier parts of Leeds.

Please Note:

Sadly, a number of breweries have closed down since the editing of this book, and information on the beers sold at certain pubs may be incorrect. Wherever Vaux and Wards beers are shown there will be other beers on sale. The same may apply to pubs selling beers from Morrell, Mitchell, Butterknowle, Ruddle, and Morland. This does not change the quality of crawls affected. If you want to help save traditional breweries and beer styles, join CAMRA – email camra@camra.org.uk

MAP

1

ABERDEEN

Aberdeen, the Granite City, is an ancient town that received its first royal charter in the 12th century, although the modern city with its handsome Union Street dates from 1806. It is Scotland's largest fishing port and home base of the North Sea oil industry. Twenty-five years ago there was little real ale here, but plenty of good pubs dotted the map. Now there is an abundance of real ale and there are more good pubs than ever before.

This circular pub crawl around the eastern end of the city starts at the bus and railway stations. One advantage of this crawl is that it can be cut if time is limited, for you are never very far from the start and finish. Most of the pubs on this crawl are open all day, usually up to midnight. Variations are indicated.

Leave the stations and turn right along Guild Street towards the harbor. Pass two pubs and the Tivoli Theatre, now closed after being a bingo hall, and cross over Market Street at the traffic lights. Twenty yards along Trinity Quay there is the busy harbor on your right, mostly packed with supply vessels servicing the oil platforms, the ferry terminal, and the occasional fishing boat. On your left is ❦The Moorings (1)❦, built in 1870 on the former site of a 16th-century coaching inn with its mermaid pub sign remaining. It sells Caledonian Deuchars IPA and 80/-, Isle of Skye Red Cuillin, and guest beers mainly from Scottish independent breweries. Toasties and snacks are available. This haven for Rock'n'Ale fans has one of the best rock jukeboxes you'll find anywhere. And with live bands most weekends, this can make for a noisy pint; but

Below: *The Moorings.*

it is well worth the effort. Three different color schemes applied during a recent paint make-over are interesting for interior decorators!

Turn left as you leave the pub and follow Trinity Quay. Take the first left, Ship Row, a cobbled road that climbs past the Maritime Museum, housed in a new extension to one of Aberdeen's oldest buildings — Provost Ross House. Follow the road up the hill with the impressive clock tower looming on the skyline. The road bears right into Exchequer Row and becomes Castle Street a few yards on. You'll pass the **Tilted Wig**, well worth a visit for its good beers, reasonably priced food, and the comfiest bar stools in the city.

Just a few yards further on, situated on the corner of Castlegate, is ❚**Old Blackfriars (2)**❚. Beers on sale are Belhaven 80/- and St. Andrews, Caledonian Deuchars IPA and 80/-, and guests. It was twice voted local CAMRA Pub of the Year and is an excellent combination of old and new. It sits on a split level and flaunts the imaginative use of stained glass and various relics, including an ancient solid wooden door in the upper level. Great value food is served all day up to 9 P.M. (8 P.M. on weekends). It opens at 10:30 A.M. for coffee and newspapers, except on Sunday.

Top: *Old Blackfriars.*

Bottom: *Blue Lamp.*

The Castlegate is a large, open, paved area and is the site of the Mercat Cross. Admire the impressive Salvation Army Citadel, with its fairytale-like tower, at the eastern end of Castlegate. On the adjacent corner to Old Blackfriars is a former bank now converted into a Wetherspoon's pub called *Archibald Simpson's*. It offers a varied selection of beers, good value food, and a long walk to the toilets! Walk west along Castle Street, passing the Tollbooth — now housing the Civic History Museum — and the Sheriff's Courts. Continue until you reach the traffic lights at the junction with Broad Street, then turn right and admire the imposing gothic structure of Marischal College. At the next set of traffic lights the road name changes to Gallowgate. Carry on along the road for two hundred yards, passing another set of traffic lights until you reach the ❚**Blue Lamp (3)**❚, easily spotted by the very large police lamp outside. There is a large, cavernous lounge, which hosts live bands usually on Friday and Saturday nights, and in which Caledonian Deuchars IPA and 80/- are sold. There is also a small, intimate public bar that dispenses guest beers. Both the original 45s jukebox in the public and the modern CD one in the lounge are free, dispelling the myth of the mean Aberdonian. It is open until 1 A.M. Friday and Saturday (must be in the pub by midnight).

Retrace your steps down Gallowgate until you reach the second set of traffic lights and turn right down Upper Kirkgate. Cross over and walk down Flourmill Lane to take a look at Aberdeen's oldest building, Provost Skene House, described as the "jewel in the city." Continue to the end of the lane and turn right into Netherkirkgate. Take the footpath between Marks and Spencer and the underpass. The footpath comes out into a piazza, and opposite is St. Nicholas Lane, where the ❦ **Prince of Wales (4)** ❦ is located. One of the first things you will notice as you enter this pub is the length of the bar counter — the longest in Aberdeen. It is adorned with a bank of eight handpumps, backed by two fine old gantries, from which Draught Bass, Caledonian 80/-, Theakston Old Peculier, Tomintoul XXX, and guest beers are sold. The Draught Bass and beers from a selected Scottish brewer are usually on offer at a special price. There is good value food every lunchtime until 2 P.M. On Sunday it opens at 11 A.M. (no alcohol till 12:30 P.M.), serving an all-day Scottish breakfast (forget any thoughts of slimming diets). Regular folk music sessions are held on Sunday evening.

From here turn right and walk to the end of St. Nicholas Lane, then use the steps on Correction Wynd to climb to Union Street. Walk 50 yards west past St. Nicholas Churchyard and take the first right up Back Wynd, then turn left into Little Belmont Street, where ❦ **Cameron's Inn (5)** ❦, known affectionately as Ma's, is located. At Aberdeen's oldest pub, the beer range varies, but usually found are Orkney Dark Island and guest beers. The private room, or "snug," on the right, with a serving hatch to order beer, is probably the oldest, most unspoiled bar in Aberdeen. At the back is a large, modern lounge where lunch and early evening meals are served. Real ale is available in both bars, but the snug is the recommended place to sample the local atmosphere with your pint.

Right next door to Ma's is the **Old Town School**, a Hogshead pub. This is worth a quick visit to see the city's only gravity-dispensed beer and to pop up to the balcony to have a look into the "cellar." On leaving, turn right towards Belmont Street and left back on to Union Street. Turn right, crossing over Union Bridge, although you'll hardly notice that you are on a bridge thanks to the skills executed by city architects more than 200 years ago. On your right you can see the imposing His Majesty's Theatre in the distance. Walk past the statue of Edward VII at the junction with Union Terrace and carry on walking west until just before you reach the splendor of the Music Hall with its pillared entrance, at which point you have the cobbled South Silver Street on your right. Walk north across Golden Square, passing the statue of George, Duke of Gordon, who was the first Colonel of the 92nd Gordon Highlanders. Continue into North Silver Street and there, underneath the Bon Accord Auction Saloons, you will find the cellar bar ▮**Under The Hammer (6)**▮. This pleasant, one-room wine bar is handy for His Majesty's Theatre. Have a seat at a table, where candles add to the intimate atmosphere, or stand at the bar and consume your pint, a perfectly acceptable practice. Caledonian Deuchars IPA and a guest beer are on offer. The bar does not open until late afternoon except on Saturday, when it opens at 2 P.M.

Below: The Grill.

Retrace your steps to Union Street and almost opposite you is ▮**The Grill (7)**▮, which is very handy during concert intermissions at the Music Hall. Boddington's Bitter, Caledonian 80/-, McEwan 80/-, and a guest beer are sold at this superb example of an Edwardian pub with unique wood panelling and a high ceiling spoiled only by the strip lighting. It also has an amazing range of malt whiskies. A variety of good value snacks are served, and there are discounts for seniors. This was one of the original men-only bars, but now there are ladies' toilets at ground-floor level. Stairs have been cleverly built where the gents' toilets used to be, leading to new downstairs facilities.

4

Leave the Grill by the back door and cross the street to *Macandrews.* This was Aberdeen's first Scottish theme bar. The concept is not as bad at it sounds, for the theme was that it only sold beers from Scottish breweries. Walk south down Crown Street, passing the flamboyant old post office building until you have the Brentwood Hotel on your left. ❦**Carriages (8)**❦ is in the cellar of the hotel. This is a very friendly, busy bar with 10 handpumps dispensing a usually excellent choice of guest ales as well as Boddington's Bitter, Caledonian Deuchars IPA, Castle Eden Ale, Courage Directors, and Flowers Original. There is also a range of bottled Belgian and German Weisse beers. Food is available in the bar with a separate restaurant open in the evening. The bar closes in the afternoons.

Retrace your steps north up Crown Street and turn right into St. John's Place. Turn left into Crown Terrace, following the signs to Bridge Street, then walk down the flight of steps to South College Street from where the bus and railway stations are only about one hundred yards away.

2

ARUNDEL

This historic small town is dominated by its magnificent castle, home to the Duke of Norfolk. The Museum of Curiosity is worth visiting to see an amazing collection of Victorian whimsy.

Bus number 702 from Brighton (via Worthing and Littlehampton) or from Portsmouth takes you to the bus station, which is a good place to start the crawl. Train travellers on the Brighton to Portsmouth line should change at Ford. From the station walk along the Causeway, pass the Arundel Park Hotel (no real ale), cross the busy A27 at the pedestrian lights, and head into town.

Above: *Swan Hotel.*

The **₹Swan Hotel (1)₹** is a large, white Victorian building situated on the corner of High Street and River Road. This lively pub is the brewery tap for Arundel Brewery and, although it is not owned by them, it sells the full range of its current portfolio together with one or two guest ales. There is only one bar, which makes it an ideal meeting place. A good selection of food is available in the bar, and there is a restaurant attached.

On leaving the Swan turn left past the Red Lion and the tourist information center, then turn left again along Tarrant Street until you reach, on your left, **₹The Eagle (2)₹** on the corner of the mouth-wateringly-named Brewery Hill. It is a popular and basic pub with one large bar and an annex. The beers on sale are Draught Bass, Fuller's London Pride, and Courage Directors Bitter.

A little further along Tarrant Street, on the corner of Kings Arms Hill, you should not be entirely surprised to find the **₹King's Arms (3)₹**. This old, established free house dating from 1625 was the local CAMRA branch Pub of the Year in 1997. It is certainly one that you should not miss. There are two bars with a range of four ales, always in excellent condition. Regular beers are Fuller's London Pride and Young's Special; Hopback beers are also usually available. The accent is on beer, so the food menu tends to be basic. There is often Morris dancing on summer evenings.

Leave the King's Arms and walk up the hill, which is short but has an increasing gradient. Then cross Maltravers Street and ascend Parsons Hill, turning left at the Roman Catholic cathedral and continuing along London Road to ♥**St. Mary's Gate Inn (4)**♥. The sign on the pub misleadingly proclaims "free house" on what is in fact a Hall and Woodhouse pub selling Badger beers. The beers are well kept, and the pub is friendly and popular with diners. It was built in 1525 as a farm dwelling and is well worth visiting for its historical significance.

On leaving what most folks call the Mary Gate, aim for the White Hart by going back into town towards the castle along

London Road and then down High Street alongside the imposing castle walls. It is a fair walk from the Mary Gate, and you may be tempted to try *The Norfolk Hotel (5)* and *The Red Lion (6)* on the way. The Norfolk is a cozy, oak-panelled pub selling three real ales, although it is not primarily a cask-ale-oriented bar. The Red Lion is a strange "A" shape with an

Top: *Drinking in view of the castle.*

Right: *St. Mary's Gate Inn.*

island bar that sells Ind Coope Bitter, Young's Special, and Ansell Bitter, which are usually well kept.

Cross the river at Queen Street and find ❦**The White Hart (7)**❦ on your immediate left. It is a free house, and the range of beers is constantly changing. The only general rule is that it tends to sell Gales during the winter months and a wider choice in the warmer weather (Hopback Summer Lightning sometimes). The bar is very comfortable and the hosts are friendly. First impressions might say that the decor is a bit fussy or overcrowded with bric-a-brac, but the quality of the beer soon compensates for this. Rational people might at this point decide to stagger back to the starting point. If you do not fall into this category, or only drink halves and enjoy a mile-long walk, then turn right as you leave the White Hart, going over the bridge and right again, following Mill Road to its end. You will pass Swanbourne Lake, which is a wild-bird sanctuary (although Southern Water does its best to prevent this in summer), before reaching ❦**The Black Rabbit (8)**❦ to enjoy another selection of Hall and Woodhouse's Badger beers, usually Dorset Best, Dorset IPA, and Tanglefoot as well as a house beer, Black Rabbit Bitter. This pretty riverside pub — the only one in Arundel — is one mile from the town center. The walking time is up to 20 minutes. A picturesque route affording dramatic views of the castle is along the riverbank, but this is less direct and doubles the walking time. It is also not recommended at night.

3

BATH

Bath is a city of mainly Georgian elegance with many well-preserved buildings, including the 18th-century Assembly Rooms, the Guildhall, the fashionable terraces, Bath Abbey, and the Roman Baths. The cultural quality of the city is reflected in its pubs, as you shall see.

From Bath Spa railway station or the bus station head up through the center of the city to the **🍺Old Green Tree (1)🍺** in Green Street. This is a charming, three-room pub, and both the wood-panelled front and back rooms are non-smoking. The Uley Brewery brews a house beer, and others include Pitchfork from the RCH brewery, Wickwar BOB, and a porter. The pub does not open until 7 P.M. on Sunday.

From Green Street cross over Milsom Street into Quit Street, and then go to **🍺Hatchets (2)🍺** in Queen Street. This is a very popular, genuine free house with the beers always changing, even on a daily basis, but they are always well kept, well served, and reasonably priced. Go back to Milsom Street and head up to the traffic lights at the bottom of the hill on Landsdown Road.

"Oh! Who can ever be tired of Bath?"

Jane Austen

If you feel like a brisk walk, make your way up the hill to the **🍺Old Farmhouse (3)🍺**, a lively Wadworth house with a single horseshoe bar and superb views over the city. Look for the portrait of the landlord on the pub sign. Apart from Wadworth ales there are also Butcombe Bitter, Draught Bass, and Abbey Bellringer. Behind the pub you'll find the home of Abbey Ales, Bath's only brewery.

Head downhill via Guinea Lane to **🍺The Star (4)🍺**, a classic city-center, two-room pub full of atmosphere. Draught Bass is served from glass pitchers filled by gravity from the cask. Other beers include Exmoor Ale, Wadworth 6X, and a guest ale.

A hundred yards away at the top of Walcot Street is the **🍺Hat and Feather (5)🍺**, a noisy pub that is popular with aging hippies, who come for the live music, and students, who dominate the table football machine. Drinks include Courage Bitter and Directors, Smiles Best Bitter, and Cheddar Valley cider.

Down from the Hat and Feather in Walcot St. is ❦The Bell Inn (6)❦, an open-plan bar that is renowned for its live music (folk, jazz and rock) and an excellent range of beers including Courage Bitter and Directors, Exmoor Gold, Fuller's London Pride, Smiles Best Bitter, and Exhibition. There is an outdoor drinking area.

Make your way to Saracen Street and the ❦Pig and Fiddle (7)❦. This is an Ashvine outlet that was recently refurbished and extended. Very lively and popular with the twenty-somethings of Bath, it is just the place to be on a balmy summer evening and the right place to end a crawl. Try Ashvine Bitter, Challenger, Hop and Glory,

Top: *The Old Green Tree.*

Bottom: *The Star Inn.*

a guest beer, and Thatcher's cider. It's downhill from here to the stations.

MAP

4

BELFAST

Belfast is one of the great Victorian cities. It has an economic base in shipbuilding and manufacturing textiles, especially linen.

Start the crawl from the Europa Bus Centre. Go through the Great Northern Mall into Great Victoria Street, and facing you are the first two pubs on the crawl. To the right is the **▮Beaten Docket (1)▮**, a modern, lively pub with a public bar on the ground floor and a comfortable lounge and restaurant upstairs. There is a non-smoking area, and children are welcome. It has what is probably the best selection of real ales in Northern Ireland, including Draught Bass, Cain's FA, Caledonian Deuchars and IPA, Tomintoul Laird's Ale, and guests. There is live music on Friday and Saturday evenings.

Next door is the **▮Crown Liquor Saloon (2)▮**, one of the best known and best loved pubs in Ireland. The Crown is one of the great gin palaces of the world. It sells Draught Bass and a fine selection of wines and spirits, and the food has a high reputation. It is owned by the National Trust and managed by Bass Ireland. It was built in 1826 as the Railway Tavern to service the fledgling Belfast to Lisburn line. Its new name came in 1885 when, to the design of the owner's son, it was rebuilt by Italian craftsmen who were in Belfast to build churches. And a century later the Trust gave it a sympathetic restoration. John Betjeman tagged it "a many-colored cavern," and his description is easy to understand. Take your time to admire it from the tiled exterior with its ornate columns and splendid iron gates. The magnificent bar with its glorious tiled backdrop faces 10 private rooms, or "confessionals," as they are called. The Crown saw through the violent times with a few scars, yet many famous folks continued to come. Ask to see the visitors book just to find out who they were.

"I was born in Belfast between the mountain and the gantries

To the hooting of lost sirens and the clang of trams."

Louis Macneice

Make your reluctant departure and turn right into Great Victoria Street, passing the Europa Hotel and the Grand Opera House into College Square. Fork right into King Street. Turn right at Castle Street and left at Chapel Lane, then turn right into Bank Street where you will find ***Kelly's Cellars (3)***. This is marked as a "try also" entry simply because you are

Top: *The Crown Liquor Saloon.*

Bottom: *Kelly's Cellars.*

unlikely to find real ale on sale here. However, you will not be disappointed, so seize the moment. The pub was built in 1720 and is the oldest continuously-licensed premises in Belfast. It has a wealth of history and played its part in the 1798 insurrection when men like Wolfe Tone, Thomas Russell, and Henry Joy McCracken met and plotted here. Famous visitors abound, particularly sportsmen: golfers Dai Rees, the winning Ryder Cup captain, and Fred Daly, the only Irishman ever to win the Open Championship; boxers such as Floyd Patterson and Sonny Liston; and great footballers Matt Busby, Bill Shankley, Stanley Matthews, and the rest of the Blackpool team that won the 1953 FA Cup. There were entertainers, too: Wilfred Pickles, G. H. Elliott, Sir John Martin Harvey, Guy Mitchell, and Buck Alec, who signed himself as "the world's greatest lion tamer." Today's customers are journalists and lawyers and "the plain people of Ireland." There have been changes over the years at Kelly's Cellars, but the essential atmosphere remains along with the barrel seats, whitewashed walls, and archways as old as the pub. Food is available at lunchtime, with a basic menu downstairs and more variety on the first floor. There is music, either traditional or blues, on the weekends, when a later opening is allowed.

Continue along Bank Street, turning right into Royal Avenue and left into Castle Place. Finally, turn left into Lombard Street for the ❦Monico Bars (4)❦. You are now in the heart of the busy shopping area of the city. Cain's FA from Liverpool is on regular sale along with some guest beers. There is a small private room, or "snug," at the front, popular with the racing fraternity, and a larger bar at the back with a number of enclosed cubicles. It is well decorated with mirrors and wood prints. Food is available at lunchtime.

Close by is our next stop. Carry on to Rosemary Street, and on the right is Winecellar Entry and ❧ **Whites Tavern (5)** ❧, which sells Cain's FA and occasional guest beers. This pub dates back to 1630 and is one of the oldest in Belfast. It was once a warehouse, and the exposed beams give it real character. The home-cooked food at lunchtime is a good value.

Retrace your steps to Rosemary Street and turn right into Bridge Street then left into High Street. After the Hipark Centre, turn right and go to the junction with Victoria Street, where you'll find ❧ **Bittles Bar (6)** ❧. This unusually shaped bar is friendly and very welcoming. It is tastefully decorated and most comfortable. There is a fine collection of watercolors of Belfast's characters and views of the city. It sells Draught Bass and Worthington White Shield in bottles and serves food at lunchtime.

Not more than a hundred yards away in Victoria Square is the ❧ **Kitchen Bar (7)** ❧. This cozy and much loved pub dates from 1859. There are cask beers from the Scottish Courage stable and also guest ales from a "cellar" that is two floors up. For its first 130 years in business it was run by the Conlon family, who created a famous relationship between the pub and the Empire Theatre, which stood next door. Many famous stars trod its boards, and the Kitchen Bar was the entertainers' pub. Charlie Chaplin appeared at the Empire as a young man, and so did Marie Lloyd, Lily Langtry, Will Fyffe, George Formby, and many others. The walls of the pub are covered with theatre posters. The long, narrow bar at the front is the popular place to be, and the parlor bar behind is a touch more upmarket, with many theatre memories on its walls. The food here is filling — good helpings of Irish stew, for example — and there is a good choice of drinks. There are also regular beer festivals. You are now about a 10-minute walk away from the starting point and perhaps another visit to the Crown!

Below:
Kitchen Bar.

5

BRIDGNORTH

Bridgnorth is one of the most idyllic market towns in Shropshire. It has fine historic buildings, including a tower that leans steeper than that of Pisa, and it is well supplied with good pubs. This crawl takes in eight of the best pubs in the town, including four that are in the *Good Beer Guide* (CAMRA, 1999). Be warned that many of the pubs close during the afternoon.

The only train access into Bridgnorth is by the Severn Valley Railway, for which a separate crawl is included beginning on page 141. Trains from Kidderminster and Bewdley run on weekends in winter and throughout the week from the end of May to the beginning of October. Bus services to the town run from several surrounding towns; it is best to seek travel advice from the companies, Midland Red and Go Whittle. Bus termini are indicated on the crawl.

This is a cirular crawl and can be joined at any point, but for convenience the Severn Valley Railway station is used as the starting point. Leaving one of the great delights, the Railwayman's Arms, until the end, walk down to Hollybush Road to the **⏏Hollyhead Inn (1)⏏**, which shares a parking lot with the railway. Cask beers on sale include Draught Bass, Fuller's London Pride, Boddington's Bitter, and a guest ale. This tastefully renovated pub was once called the George Hotel and has a small bar and comfortable lounge with a separate dining area. There are many exposed beams and a cozy, open fireplace. A patio at the front is served directly from a hatch to the lounge bar. Meals are served at lunchtime in a separate restaurant. Children are welcome and the pub is disabled friendly. Overnight accommodation is available.

Continue along Pound Street up to its junction with Salop Street. Turn left, and opposite is the **⏏Bell and Talbot (2)⏏**. This is a 250-year-old former coaching inn retaining many features of its former brewhouse at the back. There are open log fires in two of the three attractive bars that sell Banks' Mild and Bitter, Cameron Strongarm, and Marston's Pedigree. There is good food, with evening meals until 8:30 P.M., but no meals on Sunday. This is a mecca for live music, with varying styles played on four nights, including Irish on Sunday. A mural in the alleyway shows musicans, staff, and customers. There are bedrooms to let. It is disabled friendly.

When you retrace your steps into Whitburn Street, on the right is the ❦Carpenter's Arms (3)❦. This single-room pub dates from 1888. Bitter and Buccaneer beers are on the hand-pumps. Food is available at lunchtime and in the early evening. There is no jukebox. The pub is wheelchair accessible.

Turn right out of the Carpenter's Arms along Whitburn Street, then turn left at High Street. Pass through the historic North Gate with its museum. It is the only one of five gates of the town's original fortifications that remains. On the left is the

❦Bear Inn (4)❦, a regular entry listed as a building of archi-tectural and historic interest in CAMRA's *Good Beer Guide* (CAMRA, 1999). There are two characterful bars, without juke-boxes or fruit machines, in which Batham's Mild and Best

Bitter, Boddington's Bitter, Ruddle's Bitter, and a constantly changing guest beer are sold. The Bear is renowned for its excellent food and is noted in Sue Nowak's *Good Pub Food* as serving food of special interest or merit. Gourmet nights on Thursday need advance book-ing. High standard accommodation is

available. Buses leave from here to Ludlow and from the nearby Golden Lion to Ludlow and Kidderminster.

Return through North Gate into High Street, and on the left find the ❦Harp (5)❦. This dynamic, black-and-white-faced building has been little altered since it was built. It was originally a wine and spirits retailer licensed as the Harp Stores. The pub is very popular, particularly with younger folks. There are two rooms and a central bar selling Banks' Mild and Bitter and Marston's Pedigree. The use of electric pumps for Banks' beers is a standard practice in line with company policy; however, it is real ale (cask beer). Food is available at lunchtime. The Harp is one of the few pubs in Bridgnorth that is open all day.

Continue along High Street, turning left into Cartway and bearing sharply to the right. On your left is the ▌**Black Boy Inn (6)**▐, known locally as the Blackie Boy (thought to indicate that a former landlord was a chimney sweep who employed young boys to climb inside chimneys to clean them). It was first licensed in 1790 and now sells Banks' Mild and Bitter and Marston's Pedigree beers. It has a bar and lounge with some old photographs of the town and a beer garden that commands wonderful views over the low town and the River Severn. Families are made most welcome. Lunch is served Monday through Saturday, and early evening meals are served on weekdays. There is disabled access.

Proceed down Cartway into Underhill Street and turn left into Bridge Street to cross the river. Immediately on the right is the ▌**Black Horse Hotel (7)**▐, also known as "Bentley's." It was built about 1800 and first licensed in 1810. There is a good selection of real ales, including Banks' Mild and Bitter; two house beers, Black Horse Best Bitter and Shire Bitter (in truth Morrells Varsity and Graduate); and a guest beer. The name is taken from the color of a horse stabled here in 1879 that is said to have gone on to win the Grand National. There

Below: *Town Hall.*

is some doubt about its name, but the stables remain. There is a front bar, lounge, and separate non-smoking restaurant. No meals are served on Sunday evenings. Accommodation is available and there is access for the disabled. Buses leave from nearby to Wolverhampton, Madeley, Telford, and Wellington.

It is a fair walk now to the final stop, but it is very picturesque. Recross the bridge and turn left on Underhill Street, passing the caves and the information board at the foot of the cliff. The caves once stored locally brewed beers before they were bottled and transported by river. Follow the road around and up New Road, then cross the

footbridge to the railway station.

The ❦**Railwayman's Arms (8)**❦ is the former waiting room and is on the platform of the northern terminus of the Severn Valley Railway. This is another regular entry in the *Good Beer Guide* (CAMRA, 1999) and is the home of the Bridgnorth branch of CAMRA. In addition to Batham's Best Bitter, there are three regularly changing guest beers from small independent breweries and a good range of malt whiskies. The bar is full of railway memorabilia, or "railwayana," as the aficionados call it. More about the Severn Valley Railway can be found on the crawl that begins on page 141.

Above and right: *The Railwayman's Arms.*

6

BRISTOL

Bristol is a seafaring city that grew over several centuries on a natural harbor in the River Avon. Over the years it has served the wool, slave, and wine trades amongst many others. It was here that the phrase "paying on the nail" originated. Civil engineer and naval architect Isambard Kingdom Brunel's association with the city continues in many ways: the Clifton Suspension Bridge, the docks that he redesigned, the Great Western Railway, and ships including the SS Great Britain, which is now in its original dock. There are also many wonderful old buildings, such as the cathedral, which began life as a 12th-century Augustinian abbey.

This is a linear crawl that starts from Bristol Temple Meads Railway Station and finishes at Bristol Bus Station, or the Centre. Or it can just as easily start at the bus station: take all the directions in reverse and finish back at the railway station. The choice is yours! Both ends are linked by frequent bus services.

Bristol Temple Meads Railway Station, one of Brunel's greatest achievements, was built during the construction of the Great Western Railway. Walk down the station approach and cross the busy main road at the bottom. Immediately across the road, you will see the ❚**Reckless Engineer (1)**❚, a wooden-floored alehouse well noted for its support of local and regional real ale breweries. Between two and five traditional beers are normally available, and the pub is usually open all permitted hours, although it may close on Saturday afternoons, depending on football schedules. There is occasional live music — a CAMRA membership card guarantees free entry!

From here go back across the road, bearing left across the roundabout towards Victoria Street. Once there look for the ❚**Kings Head (2)**❚ on the right. This was described as a "friendly Victorian gem" in the *Good Beer Guide* (CAMRA, 1999) and is well worth a visit. It has a superb private room, or "snug," and dispenses beers from the Courage and Bass/ Worthington range.

Turn right and carry on walking into nearby Temple Street. Note Temple Church with its leaning spire (Bristol's answer to

"There were three sailors of Bristol City

Who took a boat and went to sea.

But first with beef and captain's biscuits

and pickled pork they loaded she."

William Makepeace Thackeray

the Leaning Tower of Pisa!) on the right. Once in Temple Street, look carefully for the ♥**Cornubia (3)**♥, which is set back on the left side, opposite the fire station. Cornubia only reopened to the public in 1996 after many years as the hospitality pub for the nearby Courage Brewery. It is a small pub with sometimes restricted opening hours, so do check first. Four ales are normally on sale, usually from local independent brewers. There is a small and popular restaurant where booking is essential.

On leaving the pub, keep left along Temple Street, then turn right (taking care to avoid any fire engines!) into Counterslip, leading over the river (known as the Floating Harbour) into Passage Street. Almost immediately on your left, you will see the aptly named ♥**Bridge Inn (4)**♥. This takes beer from the Bath Ales brewery, as well as Courage, and has been a *Good Beer Guide* regular for many years. It also claims to be Bristol's smallest bar, as you will see!

After enjoying a pint here, you now have a 10-minute walk in front of you. Turn right and retrace your steps back across the river, but keep straight, passing Courage's Bristol Brewery. At the junction with Victoria Street, turn right and cross the river again at Bristol Bridge, then bear left into Baldwin Street. On the right, you will soon notice the ♥**Old Fish Market (5)**♥, Fuller's first pub in Bristol, and one of its first anywhere outside London. It opened in 1997 and is tastefully decorated inside. It sells the full range of Fuller's beers and some guest ales from time to time.

Turn left on leaving here and you will soon come across steps on your left leading up to the St. Nicholas Market area. The market itself offers stalls selling a very wide range of products and is great to browse in if you want a break from the serious business of drinking. A path leads straight through the market area and ends up in the pedestrianized area of Corn Street. This is one of the oldest parts of Bristol and is famous for the term "pay on the nail," for traders from the Corn Exchange settled their bills here. The "nails" themselves, four bronze pillars, can still be seen.

From here, look left and you will see a road. Walk into this from the pedestrianized area, and on the right you will see one of Bristol's finest pubs, the ♥**Commercial Rooms (6)**♥, owned by J. D. Wetherspoon. It was extensively and very expensively (costing well over £1 million) renovated from a gentlemen's club. It won the English Heritage/CAMRA award for refurbishment in 1996. It is a large pub, which can get very busy in the evenings, and stocks the usual range of ales that the company is well known for at competitive prices. There are occasional beer festivals.

Next door on the right is a "try also" entry, the *Wig and Pen (7)*. This underwent a recent conversion, and it's worth popping inside to view the interior. A range of beers mainly from Morlands is on sale. Like the Commercial Rooms, this pub can get very busy on weekends.

From the Wig and Pen, turn right and then right again into St. Stephen's Street, which leads into the wide expanse that is the Centre. Keep to the right, and a short distance away on the right is the ♥**White Lion Hotel (8)**♥. This is a small pub where you can watch the hustle and bustle of the traffic circulating the one-way system (a bus spotter's paradise!). It sells a range of ales, often from regional and independent brewers.

On leaving the White Lion, bear right and cross the Centre at the pedestrian lights. Bear to the right and you will arrive at the ♥**Three Sugar Loafs (9)**♥, a split-level pub selling beers from the Moles range. Opposite the pub is an excellent fish-and-chip shop.

Between the pub and the chip shop are the Christmas Steps. Walk up these, noting the range of antique shops and antiquarian booksellers on either side. At the top of the steps cross straight over Colston Street and walk up Lower Park. A one-minute walk will bring you to the ♥**Ship (10)**♥, which sells a range of ales including beers from independents and regionals. Many nautical artifacts are on display in this two-level pub.

Retrace your walk to Colston Street and cross over it, then bear left and walk for a couple of minutes. You will then see the ❦**Smiles Brewery Tap (11)**❦ on your right. This wonderfully designed pub serves the full Smiles range and occasional guest beers. When originally opened, the bar area was the size of the pub — very small! It is only in the last few years that it has been expanded to give much-needed room. The brewery is right behind and below the pub.

The crawl is now at an end. If you turn left out of the pub and walk back down Colston Street, you will come back to the Centre, from where most Bristol First City Line bus services depart, as well as some country First Badgerline services. You can catch buses back to Temple Meads Station from several locations. Or you can turn right on leaving the Brewery Tap into Upper Maudlin Street (passing the large Bristol Royal Infirmary on the left) then right into Lower Maudlin Street, bearing left for the bus station proper. If you are doing the tour in reverse, buses depart next to the Reckless Engineer pub for the Centre and bus station.

7

BURTON UPON TRENT

Nowhere in the world is better known for its brewing heritage than Burton upon Trent. Towns like Milwaukee, Pilsen, Munich, and Copenhagen are small-fry in comparison.

This crawl takes you through the industrial heart of the town past the two giant breweries (now both owned by Bass) to pubs of great character where beers from all the town's breweries, and further afield, can be tasted. A visit to the town should, if possible, include the splendid Bass Museum.

The best place to start is the railway station. Unfortunately, whichever way you follow this crawl, a certain amount of backtracking is involved, but it's well worthwhile. From Burton station turn right down Station Street to the first stop on the corner of Mosley Street. ❦**The Roebuck (1)**❦, known locally as the "Ale House," stands opposite the former Ind Coope brewery now known as Bass "C." (The Bass brewery is Bass "B." And before you ask whatever happened to Bass "A," "C" is for Carlsberg-Tetley and "B" is for Bass!) The beers include Greene King Abbot, Draught Burton Ale, Marston's Pedigree, Morland Old Speckled Hen, Tetley Bitter, and guests that are usually from a small, independent brewer. The single bar is popular with brewery workers. "Breweryana" and related prints and artifacts are displayed on the walls. There is bar billiards and piped music — sometimes a little too loud! The pub is a regular entry in the *Good Beer Guide* (CAMRA, 1999).

Turn right along Station Street to the ❦**Devonshire Arms (2)**❦, a Grade II listed building. There is a small front bar and a large, comfortable lounge. This recently became the third tied house of the Burton Bridge Brewery, and its trade and reputation are building up steadily. On sale are three Burton Bridge beers (usually Bridge Bitter, a dark beer, and perhaps the monthly special) and Draught Burton Ale. Of particular interest is the 1850s town map that shows the locations of many of Burton's lost breweries.

Continue along Station Street and look through the railings on the right at the Bass (B!) brewery to see an unusual fountain made entirely of metal beer casks. Backtrack, turn left into

"Say, for what were hop-yards meant,

Or why was Burton built on Trent?

Or many a peer of England brews

Livelier liquor than the Muse,

And malt does more than Milton can

To justify God's ways to man."

A. E. Housman

Top: *Coopers Tavern.*

Center: *Black Horse.*

Bottom: *Thomas Sykes.*

Cross Street, and proceed to ▮**Coopers Tavern (3)**▮ on the right. This is a traditional alehouse with a counterless back taproom. Draught Bass, Hardy and Hanson's Best Bitter and Classic, and Marston's Pedigree are sold. Stillaged casks (cooled in summer), barrel tables, and a "top bench" seat in the corner are all of interest. The taproom oozes character but can get smoky. The less traditional lounge is a retreat from the fog. There is good, reasonably priced, wholesome food served in a very friendly environment.

From here go to the junction with Moor Street, then turn right and walk a hundred yards or so to the ▮**Black Horse (4)**▮, an honest-to-goodness, two-room local. This pub is one of the best (consistently good) Pedigree outlets in Marston's hometown. The basic bar is dominated by a pool table and darts and other pub games played by the enthusiastic locals. The lounge is cozy with old photographs of the locality on the walls.

Cross the road and walk straight ahead past the roundabout into Anglesey Road until you reach the ▮**Thomas Sykes (5)**▮. The pub is situated on the site of the former Everard's Brewery, part of which became the now sadly defunct Heritage Brewery Museum. The pub is in the former stables and wagon sheds of the brewery. It comprises two high-ceilinged rooms with stable fittings and "breweryana," wooden benches, and cobbled floors and is truly atmospheric. Beers on sale are Draught Bass, Marston's Pedigree and Owd Roger, and two guest beers. The now derelict brewery was built in 1880 by Thomas Sykes of Liverpool and was owned by Everards between 1898 and 1984. It was a fine example of a tower brewery, but it is now in a ruinous state. Note the Goat Maltings behind the brewery buildings with the eponymous weathercock.

Backtrack down Anglesey Road and cross the roundabout. Turn right into Moor Street and left up Mosley Street, which

Above: *The Alfred.*

returns you to Station Street. Turn left into Borough Road and pass the railway station, then turn right into Derby Street. The final call, ♥ **The Alfred (6)** ♥, is on the left after a 5 to 10-minute walk from the station. This is Burton Bridge Brewery's second tied house. It sells a wide variety of their beers including XL, Bridge Bitter, Porter, Festival Ale, seasonal beers, and a guest. It has spartan, bare boards, though with pleasant seating and a raised eating lounge, it is full of character. A game room with bar billiards, table football, and other games is at the back. Families are welcome and budget-priced bed and breakfast is available.

MAP

8

BURY ST. EDMUNDS

A historic market town named after the last king of East Anglia, Bury St. Edmunds is of much interest. Visit the cathedral; the Athenaeum, a one-time center of the town's social life; the Georgian theatre, the Queen Anne mansion, and the museum in a 12th-century flint and stone building. And then, of course, there are the pubs. This crawl provides a visitor with a pleasant tour of most of the historic sites.

Start from the public parking lot behind ❦**The Fox (1)**❦; take a footpath to the pub. This fine pub full of character claims to be the oldest in the town. Originally it consisted of only the rear part with its superb, oak-panelled room, but it has since been expanded. It sells Greene King ales (IPA, Abbot, and seasonal ales) and has a reputation for good food.

Leave the Fox and walk via Mustow Street, following the old abbey wall. Turn left into the Abbey Gardens for a pleasant stroll with views of the cathedral (soon to have a new tower) and exit by the Abbey Gate into Angel Hill. Turn left at the gate and go past the front entrance of the cathedral. View Norman Tower before turning right into Churchgate Street,

where you'll find the ❦**Queen's Head (2)**❦. This is a free house with a Victorian facade on an older building. Popular with younger folk, it is quite large with a patio and conservatory at the rear. Adnams Bitter and Broadside, Nethergate IPA, and frequently changing guest beers are available along with a limited food menu.

Above:
Queen's Head.

From here turn into Bridewell Lane, which, typical of this part of the town, has many fine timber-framed buildings. A house named "The Blackbirds" was formerly a pub. Turn left into Tuns Lane (yes, a pub called the "Three Tuns" formerly occupied 44 Crown Street) and then right for views of St. Mary's Church and Great Churchyard. Continue along Crown Street, passing the *Dog and Partridge* (interesting front bar if you have time to linger) with Greene King brewery premises on either side until you enter Westgate Street. Opposite is the Theatre Royal, the only theatre in the country owned by the National Trust. The Georgian auditorium is open for viewing when no performance is on. Continue to the right along Westgate Street, passing the recently closed maltings, to the ▮**Rose and Crown (3)**▮, an unspoiled town pub owned by Greene King. There are two bars and an off-sales area between them. IPA, Abbot, XX Dark (mild), and seasonal beers are available along with good value food and accommodation.

From the Rose and Crown enter Whiting Street and walk towards the town center, passing several more fine timber-framed buildings on the way. Cross Churchgate Street, viewing the Essex boarded ***Mason's Arms*** on the right. Carry on to the top of Whiting Street, then turn left towards the imposing Corn Exchange, and neatly tucked away to the right you will

find the country's smallest pub, ▮**The Nutshell (4)**▮, in the Traverse. This is one not to miss, so do not go on Sunday, for both this and the next entry will be closed. Its uniqueness is registered in the Guinness Book of Records. Yet another Greene King house selling IPA and Abbot, it is full of curios, including a mummified cat found interned in a wall.

Leaving the Nutshell with the Corn Exchange on your left, follow the pedestrianized Traverse to ▮**Cupola House (5)**▮, reputedly the oldest townhouse in Bury. It has fine oak panelling to admire and a superb cupola on top. Yet another Greene King pub with IPA and Abbot on sale, it has good value food with early morning breakfasts available on market days.

Carry on from the Cupola House along the Traverse to enter the Cornhill, which is Bury's busy marketplace on Wednesday and Saturday. The handsome Moyses Hall in the corner to

Above: *Angel Hotel.*

the right houses a fine museum of local treasures. Follow along the extended market area, turn right into the Buttermarket, and enter the top of Abbeygate Street, from where you can see the Abbeygate at the bottom of the hill. Walk down Angel Hill and turn right to enter the ♦**Angel Hotel (6)**♦. This is the last surviving town hotel. This vine-covered, superb building dominates Angel Hill. It has all the characteristics of a first-class hotel, including the prices! Adnams Bitter and a guest beer are on sale. The Angel has Dickensian associations — he gave readings here and used it as a location in Pickwick Papers.

From the Angel retrace your steps through the Abbey Gardens to the parking lot, but beware that the gardens close at dusk, so an alternative route skirting around the abbey to the left of the Abbey Gate may be necessary.

MAP

9

CAMBRIDGE

There is much to see in this ancient city, not only the colleges but the museums, the churches, the Backs, and the Botanic Gardens. The pub crawl starts at Cambridge Bus Station in Drummer Street in the center of town. It is the depot for National Express coaches and the pickup and drop-off point for the bus circular to the railway station.

Begin by following Emmanuel Street down to St. Andrew's Street, then turn left with Emmanuel College on your left. You will pass **The Castle (1)**, a pub owned by Greene King with a limited range of real ale and a rather cramped and dingy interior. It does have a colorful history, however. There is an interesting story about how Doctor Barnes, a senior university tutor, introduced a £20 "shag tax" penalizing any freshmen found intoxicated. When the Sherwoods, the university's drinking society, was banned by this same tutor, the landlord of the Castle announced that its members were welcome to seek refreshments at his establishment. Since then there has been a tradition of hanging photographs of the current year's membership of the society on the pub's walls.

"We were walking the whole time — out of one college into another…I felt I could live and die in them and never wish to speak again."

Mary Lamb

The first stop is the ▮**Fountain Inn (2)**▮ in Regent Street. Housed within a Victorian building, it has a traditional wooden interior with bare wooden floorboards. It has one long bar running three-quarters of the length of the pub and an open-plan seating area. The front of the pub has a large, traditional, leaded bay window that gives great views of the street and the University Arms Hotel opposite. The selection of real ales is good, including Theakston Best Bitter, XB, Old Peculier, Courage Directors, Charles Wells Bombardier, and two guest ales together with a good selection of bottled beers including Duvel, Czech Budvar, Marston's Owd Rodger, and some wheat beers. The atmosphere is lively and the staff is friendly. This place is popular with the students, particularly those from Downing College next door. Food is served up to 7 P.M. with a selection of snacks, pies, and puddings — the pies are famous and include beef and ale, lamb and rosemary, and creamy vegetable and herb.

From the Fountain carry on down Regent Street, passing Downing College on your right. Either continue along Regent

Street and go down an alley and into the ▾Hogshead (3)▾, or go down Regent Terrace to get to the Hogshead by the entrance in Parker's Piece. This pub has a cellar bar with a large seating area and another large bar and seating area upstairs. The staff is very friendly and the selection of ales is good: Adnams, Young's Special, Black Sheep, Brains, Marston's Pedigree, Morland's Old Speckled Hen, Brakspear Bitter, Wadworth 6X, Atomsplitter from the local City of Cambridge brewery, and at least three guest ales. The pub affords a view across Parker's Piece — a large green area in the center of Cambridge that is popular in the summertime for lazing around or flying a kite. It is common land where residents can tether a goat. The Hogshead has a traditional barn decor. It is quite spacious and, while it can get busy, it is never really crowded.

It's now time for a pleasant stroll across Parker's Piece, weather permitting, to its east corner. Follow East Street past the police and fire stations. On the right you pass the Zion Baptist Church and Anglia Polytechnic University, which houses the Mumford Theatre. Turn left into Dover Street and visit the ▾Tram Depot (4)▾. This is a single-bar pub with mezzanine-style seating upstairs. The bar itself is fairly small and gets very busy on Friday and Saturday nights. Beers on offer are Old Original and Tiger Best from Everards; guests often include Gale HSB and one from the Adnams range. There is a reasonable selection of food served until 9 P.M.

Above: *The Tram Depot.*

Walking from the Tram Depot turn left into Adam and Eve Street and take the second right into Prospect Row for the ▾Free Press (5)▾, where a friendly welcome awaits you. This *Good Beer Guide* (CAMRA, 1999) listed pub claims to be the only completely non-smoking pub within a one hundred-mile radius. The Free Press dates from the 1840s and today has a policy of no games, music, or other interference with the proper occupation of drinking. Beers available are Greene

King Abbot, XX Dark, and True Blue from the City of Cambridge Brewery and other guests. Food is served at lunchtime and in the evenings, although last orders for food are at about 8:30 P.M., depending on how busy they are. On Saturday it is crowded for lunch, so finding a seat may be difficult. There is also a private room, or "snug," called the Lloyds Room that the landlord claims he has fitted 61 people into — you will be amazed! There is also a small beer garden.

Move along into Orchard Street for the ▮Elm Tree (6)▮, a small bar with a front-room feel, fish tanks, and wallpaper. It has a lively atmosphere and friendly people. There is live jazz on Monday and Thursday evenings. There are bar billiards and games such as Risk! and chess available upon request. The beers include Adnams Broadside, Badger Tanglefoot, Wells Eagle, and Bombardier. Filled baguettes are available at lunchtime. There is a newly opened patio garden.

A walk of maybe 10 minutes from the Elm Tree takes you down Orchard Street, where you turn right into Emanuel Street. You will pass the Wesley Methodist church, an impressive building. On the corner by the roundabout ahead is King Street, where the ▮St. Radegund (7)▮, a *Good Beer Guide* entry, is located. This pub is quite spacious and the atmosphere is relaxed, but maybe somewhat boisterous in the evenings. Regular beers are Fuller's London Pride, Adnams Bitter, and Shepherd Neame Spitfire, plus a guest. Have a look at the graffiti on the ceiling.

Carry on down King Street, passing some alms houses that were built in 1880, to ▮The Champion of the Thames (8)▮. This has an affable, gentlemen's club feel to it with dark wood panelling and leather sofas. It sells Greene King XX Dark Mild, IPA, and Abbot beers and serves food at lunchtime. According to a large sign on the front,

"This house is dedicated to those splendid fellows who make drinking a pleasure, who reach contentment before capacity and who, whatever the drink, can hold it, enjoy it and still remain gentlemen."

Above:
*Champion of
the Thames.*

This is a fitting quote to end the pub crawl! And if you wish you can take Milton's Walk alongside Christ's Pieces back to the bus station. However, if you are still up for one more, then **The Bun Shop (9)** is worth a look. This is on King Street and boasts a tapas bar, a cocktail bar, and a "fine ole Irish bar" all in the same building. Food is served all day up to 10 P.M., and there is a reasonable selection of drinks to finish the walk on — Greene King Abbot and IPA, Tetley Bitter, and Young's Special.

10

CHESTER *Wales good midervil town*

Chester's history begins with the Romans, who established a legionary fortress on the banks of the River Dee in 76 A.D. The famous Rows — two levels of shops — are well worth seeing and are unique to Chester. Visitors should search out the Roman Amphitheatre and garden and St. Werburgh's Cathedral. One should also take a walk along the walls surrounding the city. The street layout of the old Roman town remains intact, and the city center is free from intrusive traffic. Chester is a thriving and attractive business, shopping, tourist, and administration center.

Start the crawl at the railway station. Chester General Station is probably the grandest of Chester's Victorian buildings. It was built between 1847 and 1848, and the main station building is of Italianate style. Take the free bus, which runs regularly (remember to keep your ticket) from the station to the Town Hall. Tucked in the corner of Town Hall Square, beside the Forum shopping arcade entrance, is the ❦**Dublin Packet (1)**❦ pub selling good Greenall beers plus a guest. Chester Cathedral, with its breeding ravens, is close by. This is the only city center in England where ravens breed, having nested here for five years after taking a break of more than 300 years.

From the Dublin Packet turn right and walk along Northgate Street, passing Weinholt's bakery on your right, towards the Cross. This is the very center of Chester and is where the four original Roman roads met. Carry on down Watergate Street, passing number nine, "God's Providence House," the only house to survive the plague in the late 17th century. Number eleven, now "Watergates," dates from 1744 and has a crypt from 1180. Continue along Watergate Street until you reach ❦**Ye Olde Custom House (2)**❦, a 17th-century pub selling well kept Banks' Bitter and Mild, Marston's Pedigree, and Head Brewer's Choice. This pub has an oriel window that dates from 1637.

Come out the pub and walk along the alley immediately beside the pub. Continue along Weaver Street, passing the florist on your right, then cross over the road and continue along Whitefriars. At the end turn right and you will immedi-

"The tortuous wall…wanders in narrow file between parapets smoothed by peaceful generations… with rises and drops, steps up and steps down, views of cathedral tower and waterside fields, of huddled English town and ordered English country."

Henry James

ately see the **Falcon (3)**, a well preserved, 16th-century pub serving Samuel Smith Old Brewery Bitter and basic bar food. There is live jazz on Saturday at lunchtime. It is owned by a trust, which renovated it in 1980, and is leased to Smith's. It has a fascinating history; a leaflet is available to fill you in. For a period around 1878 it was a temperance house — the Falcon Cocoa House!

Turn right out of the pub and continue down Lower Bridge Street. Take note of "Tudor House" on the opposite side, said to be one of the oldest buildings in Chester. *The Olde King's Head (4)* is worth a look in. This 16th-century pub, which was a coaching house on the Holyhead route, serves Greenall beers. Continue along Lower Bridge Street until you reach the **Bear and Billet (5)**. This pub was built in 1644 and has a very colorful history. Its name is derived from the time when Russian sailors billeted there and left their vessels guarded by Bears armed with sticks. Regular beers are Lees Bitter, one from the Theakston range, and at least one guest.

Top: *Falcon.*

Bottom: *Bear and Billet.*

From here, cross the road and walk alongside the River Dee a little way until you reach the "Recorder Steps," erected in 1700, which take you up onto the walls. Turn right and walk until you reach a fingerpost that directs you to Eastgate; continue until you see the **Albion (6)** on your left. Go down the steps or the ramp and enter this little Victorian gem selling Greenall Bitter and Mild, Cain's Bitter, and a guest beer all in excellent condition. Good traditional food is served up to 8 P.M. except on Monday. There is memorabilia of the Great War on display. The Albion is a long-standing *Good Beer Guide* (CAMRA, 1999) entry.

Continue along Park Street, passing the Nine Houses on the left — these are genuine mid-17th-century almshouses

Above:
Albion.

restored from near dereliction in 1969. Six remain of the original nine. At the end of Park Street turn right into Pepper Street, then cross Souters Lane and note the Roman Amphitheatre on your right. Cross over at the lights and make your way up St. Johns Street until you come to a T-junction, from where you have two choices.

OPTION ONE: Turn right along Foregate Street, passing the main shops until you come to the subway. Take the City Road path and continue along here until you reach the Mike Melody antique shop. Go down the steps towards the canal and you will come across ❦**Old Harkers Inn (7)**❦, a converted canalside Victorian warehouse. It sells Timothy Taylor Landlord, Fuller's London Pride, Boddington's Bitter, and guest beers. There is good value food with burgers particularly praised.

From Harkers turn left and walk along the canal until you come to Seller Street, then turn right and cross over the canal and continue to the junction with Milton Street where the ❦**Union Vaults (8)**❦ is on the corner. It is a friendly local selling Plessey Bitter and Greenall Bitter. It has folk music on Sunday evenings.

Continue along Milton Street to the ❦**Mill Hotel (9)**❦. This hotel bar (accommodation is available) is welcoming and lively and sells an extensive and continually changing range of beers, mainly from independent brewers. The house beer comes from Coach House brewery. The Mill serves a good choice of reasonably priced food both at lunchtime and in the evenings. To return to the station, walk back to Seller Street and at the Union Vaults turn left into Egerton Street. Continue as far as Crewe Street, which you should follow until it reaches City Road and the station.

OPTION TWO: Turn left at the junction and pass under the Eastgate, taking note of the second most photographed clock in England after Big Ben. The Eastgate was built in 1768-69 and the Jubilee clock was added in 1897-9. Continue until you reach the National Westminster Bank, a handsome classical building from the middle of the 19th century and one of the finest in Eastgate Street. Beside the bank are some steps; climb these and walk along the row until you reach the ❦Boot (10)❦, which sells Samuel Smith Old Brewery Bitter and has a reputation for good food. It is another fine, historic pub with a fascinating history. It was a Royalist meeting place during the Civil War, a Victorian brothel, a coffeehouse, and a 1920s gambling club. There is a leaflet available with all the details.

From here continue to walk along the row toward the Cross and turn right into Northgate Street, back towards Town Hall Square. The free bus runs from here back to the railway station.

MAP

11

CIRENCESTER *Cotswolds*

There are many reasons for visiting Cirencester. It stands on the edge of the Cotswolds and is rich in history dating back to the Romans, who made it the second most important town in Britain. The town's museum has many important relics and mosaics, and there is an amphitheatre on the edge of the town. Although the countryside around Cirencester is notable for a profusion of Roman roads, the town itself has shrugged off the Roman influence in its roads, which are mainly gently curving, even to the extent of a curved Market Place. Dominating one end of this is the magnificent 15th-century parish church, looking more like a cathedral with its soaring tower. Not least of Cirencester's attractions are the pubs, as you shall see.

The town's railway has long since disappeared, although there is still a station at Kemble, three miles outside Cirencester, on the Swindon to Gloucester line. A typically infrequent country bus service takes you from there into the Market Place. More convenient public transport is available from the National Express buses that stop in London Road outside the Beeches parking lot from where we start our tour. For those driving, this parking lot is found almost immediately on your left as you drive into Cirencester from the roundabout on what has newly become the A435, the main access to the town from the new bypass.

Below:
Waggon and
Horses.

The first stop is the ▮**Waggon and Horses (1)**▮ in London Road, just a few yards towards the town center. If you arrive by bus in the Market Place, then pick up the tour at the second pub and make this your last stop. This is a picturesque

18th-century pub with an interesting display of cameras and pump clips. It's friendly and efficient with a separate restaurant and an outdoor drinking area in a small courtyard. It sells Courage Best Bitter, Fuller's London Pride, Marston's Pedigree, Theakston Best Bitter, and Inch's Harvest cider and serves lunch and evening meals.

From London Road turn down Dyer Street and into the Market Place, always an

impressive sight, but more so on Monday and Friday, which are market days. Our next goal is the ❦**Golden Cross (2)**❦ in the wonderfully named Blackjack Street. This is a gimmick-free pub relying on friendly and efficient service and good company — appealing to all ages. There is a full-sized snooker table and a skittle alley. It is an Arkells tied house selling 2B, 3B, and the company's seasonal ales with food at lunchtime. There are two letting bedrooms including a family room. A few doors away is the fine, tiled frontage of the award-winning butcher Jesse Smith. On the other side is the excellent Corinium Museum, and across the road is the massive yew hedge of Cirencester House. For those feeling unchallenged by the relatively short stroll around the pubs, Cirencester Park is nearby in Cicely Hill.

Top: *Golden Cross.*

Bottom: *Corinium Court Hotel.*

Go through Coxwell Street and pass the antique shops of Dollar Street. Walk down the gently curving Gloucester Street to the ❦**Nelson Inn (3)**❦, a 17th-century pub with a strong nautical theme — the lounge bar is in the form of a man o' war, not nearly as bad as it sounds! It sells Wadworth 6X and a guest beer from Whitbread's selection. Meals are served at lunchtime and on weekend afternoons.

Turn back to the ❦**Corinium Court Hotel (4)**❦, which is closer to the town center. This is an upmarket hotel with a charming courtyard and garden entrances and a small flagstone bar that opens out to a smart, comfortable lounge. There is an attractive walled garden and a separate restaurant with meals at all sessions. The bars close during the afternoons. Beers on tap are Hook Norton Best Bitter, Old Hooky, Wadworth 6X, and seasonal beers. There are 16 en suite bedrooms to let.

Leaving Gloucester Street, a detour takes you past the picturesque remains of the medieval St. John's Hospital and into the Abbey Grounds. The only memory of the abbey is the Norman arched North Gate by the main road, but the lawns and lake bring welcome variety to the uninterrupted pavements of the usual pub crawl.

Return to the town center with another short detour up Castle Street. Turning left through the archway next to Oddbins brings you into a parking lot that is on the site of the old Cirencester Brewery. Further on down Cricklade Street go past the old brewery maltings. The buildings have been superbly restored, but for dwellings rather than for barley.

With a superb selection of beers and food, ▮ **The Twelve Bells (5)** ▮ in Lewis Lane is possibly Cirencester's jewel. It is a beer drinker's haven lovingly resurrected by the owner. There is a lively front bar and quieter panelled rooms at the back. The beer range varies, but there are always five on sale, including two session beers from a local brewery. Good value, high quality food is served for lunch and evening meals.

Turn right and then right again into Tower Street. Turn left into the Avenue to Chester Street and the ▮**Oddfellow's Arms (6)** ▮. This is a sensitively refurbished, back street local to which some gentle changes are promised. Beers include Greene King IPA and Abbot and guests. There is a family room and a garden. Lunches are served every day, but it is advisable to book for Sunday.

Return up Chester Street, the Avenue, and Victoria Road back to London Road, our starting point. The Waggon and Horses can be visted by those who started at the second stop, or even by those who have been here before.

12

DERBY

Derby has had many royal favors. George III gave it the right to use the Crown insignia for porcelain made there. Queen Victoria dubbed this porcelain royal, and the present queen declared Derby a city on her Jubilee visit in 1977. There were many silk mills here, and the coming of the Midland Railway in the mid-19th century and Rolls-Royce in 1908 gave Derby a firm industrial base. It is a pleasant city with many parks and a good selection of pubs.

One Tuesday in January 1997 a CAMRA survey recorded 86 different draught beers on sale in Derby. You should be luckier: The usual score is more than one hundred. The big choices are to be found in the half-dozen specialist pubs. Pubs owned by the big operators are less adventurous.

Start at the railway station, or train station, as the locals call it. There is a bit of a walk after the first two pubs, so try one and save the other for the return journey. Turn right along Railway Terrace. The housing block on the left is the world's first estate for railway workers, built for the Midland Railway in 1841 by Francis Thompson. At the end of the block on Station Approach is the flatiron-shaped ▮**Brunswick Inn (1)**▮, the world's first railway inn, built to serve the railway cottages as well as provide accommodation for the new breed of horseless travellers. It is now a free house providing a wide range of ales — as many as 17 — including those from its own brewery that opened in 1991. There are non-smoking and children's rooms; lunchtime meals are available upstairs in a time honored tradition, and the

Below:
Brunswick
Inn.

pub serves snacks all day. A beer festival is held at the end of September.

Follow the same direction and cross what used to be a bridge over the Branch Canal to the ▮**Alexandra Hotel (2)**▮ in Siddals Road. The present building, which dates from around 1870, is run by Tynemill Inns and houses a pleasant two-roomer selling Bateman's beers, Marston's Pedigree, a wide range of guest beers,

Above:
Alexandra Hotel.

and a perplexing number of bottled, continental beers. It is open all day and serves lunches and snacks. There are four reasonably priced letting bedrooms, and the breakfasts are described as "substantial." Continue along Siddals Road, which became very busy after the railway opened in 1835, as it was the quickest route out of town. Its 10 pubs must have slowed down some. The area on the left was crammed with mean houses built around courtyards, interspersed with silk manufacturers and other mills. Cross Traffic Street using the pelican crossing and continue ahead into Morledge.

The traffic roundabout on your right is believed to be the site of Derby Castle. Morledge is the old cattle market area. The bus station on the right is a nice example of 1930s design, but it will soon be swept away for something more utilitarian. On the left is the Foal and Firkin (was the White Horse), which is not part of our crawl. Cross Albert Street and walk through the sunken garden into the Market Place, dominated by the Guildhall (1842) on the left and the modern Assembly Rooms, venue for the Derby Beer Festival held in mid-July.

Cross the Market Place diagonally and take Iron Gate Street on the right. The pub on the corner — temporarily called Lafferty's — was part of a large coaching inn called the George, which housed some of the '45 rebels on the last night of their march to London. They got as far as Swarkestone the next day before turning back. Farther up on the left is a Wetherspoon's pub, the ❚**Standing Order (3)**❚, a remarkable conversion of a banking hall into a huge saloon. A little farther on the right is the cathedral of All Saints with its 15th-century tower, the rest being a rare example of Georgian ecclesiastic architecture.

At the end of the block on the right in Queen Street is the *Dolphin (4)*. This is Derby's oldest surviving pub, said to date from 1530, but most of the present building is 17th-century. The private room, or "snug," is especially pleasant, and the Bass is drinkable.

Continue up Queen Street, past John Smith's clockworks on the left. Smith was apprentice to the great Whitehurst, and the firm specializes in public clocks, with examples all over the world. Follow the road around to the left and discover the ❦Flower Pot (5)❦, home of the Headless Beer Company and an ever changing range of reasonably priced craft beers, always including a mild. It is open all day with good lunches and rolls, called "cobs," in the evening. Walk around into the backbar and see the amazing cellar. There is frequent live music in the large function room.

Retrace your steps to the Dolphin. Turn left and walk past the Silk Mill Industrial Museum and the statue of Bonny Prince Charlie around the back of the cathedral. Near the police station take Derwent Street just to the left. The Council House built in 1941 is on your right. Cross the River Derwent over Exeter Bridge. The Mansfield beers at the *Royal Standard (6)* are usually in good shape.

At the corner of Exeter Street, you'll miss a pub if you turn right. Otherwise go through the underpass, turn a sharp left, and try the ❦Peacock (7)❦ in Nottingham Road. This was a roadside inn on the main road to Nottingham. It is open all day Friday and Saturday and serves lunches and early evening meals. The diversion is worthwhile: It's probably the best Marston's Pedigree in the world, and no one has been known to leave with fewer than two pints on board.

Go back though the underpass and turn left into Exeter Street. The terrace cottage on the right was the home of Herbert Spencer, who coined the (often misunderstood and usually misattributed) phrase "survival of the fittest." The pub next door is the ❦Exeter Arms (8)❦ in Exeter Place. On the left as you enter is a delightful hearth and range enclosed by wooden settles. The beers are from Marston's and the lunchtime food is a good value. It is open all day.

Returning to the Exeter Street corner, turn right, meet up with the river, and walk under the Ring Road bridge to happen upon the ❦Smithfield (9)❦ in Meadow Road. It opened in 1869 to serve the corporation's transplanted cattle market and for much of its life was an officers' house. Now it is a locally owned free house offering a rolling range of beers along with the ubiquitous Draught Bass and Marston's Pedigree. It is open all day serving lunches and cobs.

On leaving turn right and continue down Meadow Road by the side of Northcliffe House. Cross the footbridge on the right over the river, turn left, and skirt the Holmes (now called Bass' Rec, after Michael Thomas Bass, son of a brewer and donor of the land to the borough). Cross the Mill Fleam footbridge, which will take you beneath a flyover. Turn right before the tunnel, and across two pelican crossings stands the ▮Alexandra (2)▮. After that walk you deserve a drink!

MAP

13

DUBLIN

Dublin is full of great pubs. What you will not find here is real ale, with the honorable exception of the Porterhouse (number 3 on the crawl), which brews its own. But you will find some excellent stout and lots of style and atmosphere. This crawl takes you to some of the best pubs, but in no way does it cover all of them. To cover them all takes ages. It has taken the author most of a lifetime.

If you use the DART (Dublin Area Rapid Transit), alight at Tara Street Station. After leaving it cross the road into Poolbeg Street and on the right is ❦**John Mulligan (1)**❦. It is useful to know that this pub is always known as Mulligan's of Poolbeg Street so as not to confuse it with other pubs called Mulligan's in different locations. The others, it might be said, are lesser luminaries. Soaked in literary history, the pub has been here since 1782 and has a distinct Joycean character. It is one of the best known and best loved pubs in Ireland. The attractive wooden front with its interesting windows draws you into an atmosphere of friendly conversation and good service. Many of its early days are remembered with dark, polished wooden screens, large Victorian mirrors, gas lighting, posters from the old Theatre Royal, and a general ambience of a more gentle age. One claim made on its behalf is that it serves the best pint of Guinness in Dublin. The pub stands close to some of the city's newspaper offices, and journalists have a sixth sense in sniffing out the best of drink. That many of them use Mulligan's as their watering hole is reason enough to accept the claim.

Proceed to the Quays and head west past O'Connell Bridge to Price's Lane. Turn right into Fleet Street and the ❦**Palace Bar (2)**❦, where the beer selection includes Guinness and Murphy. This pub is another favorite of newspaper people (the *Irish Times* is nearby). In more bibulous times, reporters were given their assignments in a corner of the bar known as "the intensive care unit." The place has been frequented by serious literary figures, as sketches on the wall (of James Joyce, Samuel Beckett, and Seamus Heaney) testify. The wood-panelled front bar is long and narrow and served by a counter

"The seat of this citie is of all sides pleasant, comfortable and wholesome. If you traverse hills, they are not far off. If you be delited with fresh water, the famous river called the Liffie runneth fast by. If you will take the view of the sea, it is at hand."

Richard Stanihurst

with a bank of redundant handpumps. The handsome wooden backbar is topped by old casks, copper serving jugs, and a windup gramophone. Look out for the engraved mirrors advertising Power's "pure pot still whiskey."

Above: *John Mulligan.*

Take another walk along the Quays, glancing the handsome Ha'penny Bridge, and turn left at Gratton Bridge into Parliament Street and the ❦**Porter House (3)**❦. This is one of Dublin's newest pubs, and within its capacious interior is a 10-barrel brewing plant from which a porter, two stouts, three lagers, and two Irish ales are produced. It has been created in a derelict building and has three storeys or five levels, depending which way you look at it. With a central well, it is delightfully airy and decked out in stripped pine. Look around and choose which part of the pub you want to drink or eat in. The restaurant on the first floor has a fine reputation.

Appropriately, Plain Porter has quickly established itself as one of the favorite drinks at the Porter House. It takes its name from the one-time standard drink of the Dubliners, although porter was actually a London import. In his comic novel *At Swim Two Birds,* Flann O'Brien eulogised the trend:

> When money's tight and is hard to get
> And your horse has also ran,
> When all you have is heap of debt —
> A PINT OF PLAIN IS YOUR ONLY MAN.

Another beer, a strong Irish ale called An Brainblasta, is sold by the glass. This play on words actually means "a tasty drop."

From here walk up the hill and turn left into Dame Street. On the right look for a splendid mosaic and the next stopping point, the ❦**Stag's Head (4)**❦. One of Dublin's great pubs, it is known across the world and is a favorite of business

Top: *Stag's Head.*

Bottom: *The Long Hall.*

people, tourists, and what Flann O'Brien called "the plain people of Dublin." There has been a pub on the site since 1770, but the present one dates from 1895, when it was rebuilt with loads of mahogany and etched glass mirrors in the high period of Victorian baroque. The magnificent mirrors soar up to a lofty roof, and roaring out of them is a wonderful stag's head guarding the marble-topped bar from which thousands of pints are poured each week. This is a busy pub. The main room is broken up by attractive screens and large whiskey vats that give it further appeal. Stained-glass windows also contain the stag, a handsome brute that deserves the display he gets. Food is important here, with simple but substantial fare for lunch and early evening meals. At the back is a comfortable private room, or "snug," with leather upholstery; the downstairs bar is the place for music.

Backtrack along Dame Lane and turn right into the busy South Great George's Street. Take care in crossing to the ❡**Long Hall (5)**❡, an appropriate name for a pub said to have the longest bar in Dublin. It is certainly a notable one, made of highly polished wood with an impressive inlaid brass belt and foot rail. Behind it is dispensed a fine pint of stout. A large clock displays what it claims is the "correct time." Mirrors, screens with colored glass, and fine panelling abound. A wild assortment of chandeliers lights up the rooms. The walls are full of prints showing an assortment of cartoons of politicians and caricatures of Gilbert and Sullivan characters. An archway leads to a large lounge, and on it are the names of former owners of the business. G V Hoolihan, a Kerryman, has presided here since 1973. In the 150 years of its life the Long Hall has had only four owners.

Return along the opposite side of the road to Exchequer Street and visit the ❦**Old Stand (6)**❦, which stands proudly on a busy corner. It is painted black with discrete gold lettering and has pleasant window dressings. It is a stylish pub with a dignified personality catering to locals rather than internationals. Not that visitors aren't welcome, for this is a very friendly pub. Good value roast meat lunches at reasonable prices are in demand here, and the pub has a high reputation for steaks. The screened compartments along the wall are good places to dine. There is also a smaller room at the back.

Move along Exchequer Street, which becomes Wicklow Street, and turn right into elegant Grafton Street. Enter Duke Street with ❦**Davy Byrne's (7)**❦ on the right. It has a reputation for good food and has always been experimental in its drinks policy. When Dublin toyed with cask beers in the early 1980s, Byrne's was one of the first pubs to install handpumps. Australian, Chilean, and California wines now add to the established, original range. And there is a choice of good stouts. Many people know the pub by its appearance in James Joyce's *Ulysses*. Initially the book doesn't tell us much beyond the famous enigmatic line: "He [Leopold Bloom, the book's hero] entered Davy Byrne's. Moral pub." The eponymous landlord himself appears and states his opposition to gambling. Maybe that is why his pub is moral. With three comfortable rooms catering to differing tastes, it takes its place as one of Dublin's best pubs. This is a good area for trying out other Dublin delights such as Bewley's Coffee Shop, the Gotham Café for posh pizzas, Brown Thomas and Switzer department, stores Trinity College, and the Book of Kells.

Below: O'Donoghue's.

Stroll up Grafton Street to St. Stephen's Green and take the north side, which leads into Merrion Row and ❦**O'Donoghue's (8)**❦, the home of traditional Irish music. It is where the Dubliners and many other famous musicians have gathered and played and is probably the most popular pub in Dublin. Miss it and you miss out on a cornerstone of Irish popular culture. It was built in 1789 as a grocery selling wines and spirits; it was not until 1934 that it became a pub. Its musical credentials date from the early 1960s when the Ronnie Drew Group, later to become the Dubliners, started playing there. They were followed by such names as Seamus Ennis, Dominic Behan, the Fureys, and Christy Moore. The pub was largely rebuilt after a disastrous fire in November 1985.

The long, narrow front bar has two entrances, only one of which is open at a time, depending on how busy the pub is. You must visit the place to understand! The floors are covered in Liscannor flags, and drawings of Dublin decorate the walls while high stools play sentry at the bar. The small, back snug contains a massive collection of photographs of musicians from all over the world who have played there. The scene is completed by a large covered yard with access to a food bar and the interest of many old, enamel trade signs. And whatever reason brings visitors to O'Donoghue's, it will be the great pint of Guinness that wins your vote.

Merrion Street and its continuation, Westland Row, lead you to Pearse Station, the nearest DART station.

14

DURHAM

Durham is a truly historic and beautiful city and is now one of the most popular tourist attractions in the north of England. Its magnificent nine hundred-year-old cathedral, rivalled possibly only by Lincoln's for its splendid hilltop setting, can be seen for miles around, complemented by the large and imposing castle. There are also many other ancient buildings set at various levels on the hillsides of the city. A number of these are pubs, which are well worth a visit in their own right.

Durham is well served on the main east coast railway line with fast trains to Newcastle and Scotland to the north, and York, Leeds, London, and a good many other places to the south. The station stands in a well-elevated situation a little away from the center, and the view of the castle and cathedral when emerging from here is worth an initial photograph. There is also a centrally placed bus station situated almost under the huge and impressive railway viaduct.

A good starting point is the ❦**Colpits (1)**❦, located on Hawthorn Terrace up a steepish hill out of the town. This frequent *Good Beer Guide* (CAMRA, 1999) entry sells a brew that is uncommon for the area — Samuel Smith's Old Brewery Bitter. By far the cheapest beer to be found in Durham, it sells at about two-thirds the price of most others. The pub itself, built from local stone in 1856, is a veritable time warp. The shape is basically triangular to fit in with the road junction.

"Grey Towers of Durham, yet well I loved thy mixed and massive piles. Half church of God, Half castle 'gainst the Scot."

Walter Scott

Upon leaving the Colpits, cut through Alexandra Crescent to the ❦**Old Elm Tree (2)**❦, a quiet, peaceful pub set on a steep hill named Crossgate. The pub dates from 1601, and though partially opened up, there are no really large areas. However, there is a good assortment of furniture. Beers on sale are handpumped Wards Best Bitter, Samson, Waggle Dance, and a guest beer. Food is available at lunchtime. It was Durham CAMRA Pub of the Year for 1998. Note the old-fashioned latch, or "sneck," on the outer door, the lovely cobbled road surface, and the solid stone houses opposite. Bed and breakfast accommodation is available.

Proceed further down Crossgate until a point where it swings sharply left, then visit the ❦**Fighting Cocks (3)**❦ at the nearby junction with Silver Street and South Street. This is a large

Top: *Old Elm Tree.*

Bottom: *Half Moon Inn.*

and impressive pub that has been partly opened up, yet it manages to maintain its intimate atmosphere. On sale here are Draught Bass, Stones, and Worthington Best Bitter.

To reach the fourth port of call, proceed along Silver Street, the first part of which takes you across a bridge over the River Wear before turning sharply left at its nearest point to the castle. This once busy thoroughfare has now lost most of its traffic and is all the better for being pedestrianized. Turn right into Saddler Street and look out for the ❦**Shakespeare (4)**❦ on the right. This is probably the smallest pub on the tour, but it has earned itself a "star" symbol in the *Good Beer Guide* for its delightfully unspoiled nature. It is a favorite with members of the cathedral choir. The front private room, or "snug," is particularly intimate and friendly, and a dozen or so folks make it seem crowded. The beer list includes Courage Directors, Theakston's Best Bitter, McEwan 80/-, and Webster Yorkshire Bitter, a brew now very rarely found in its former hometown of Halifax.

Rubbing shoulders with the Shakespeare is the ❦**Hogshead (5)**❦. While this pub may be fairly typical in format, it has much to commend it. The pub has a large and impressive range of real ales that includes not only the usual Boddington's Bitter, Flowers IPA, and Wadworth 6X, but also Fuller's London Pride and other guest beers. Beer prices here are rather high for the area, but the food is of good quality and not too expensive.

Now for a short, "sobering" walk. Retrace your steps a little until Elvet Bridge is seen on the right. You will shortly cross the River Wear again, but this time it is flowing in the opposite direction due to the massive curve just beyond the city center. When you reach the busy crossroads look for the ❦**Half Moon (6)**❦ at the junction of Old and New Elvet.

This is a large, split-level pub with an excellent public bar fronting onto the road. The crescent-shaped servery gives the pub its name. There are original windows and many other features of interest. The beer is Draught Bass and a guest beer from the Durham brewery. There is food at lunchtime.

Note that the former City Pub on Old Elvet is now a Scruffy Murphy, which unfortunately does not have real ale. It's a pity, for clearly this was once been a fine old pub with much character.

Continue along Old Elvet for a short distance until a tiny pub is spotted on the left, opposite a Roman Catholic church. This is the ❦**Dun Cow (7)**❦, built on the "side passage" system with two small bars, one behind the other; heavy metal tables; and outside toilets, now something of a rarity in many areas. The locals here are particularly friendly, making even a complete stranger feel immediately welcome. The beers on sale regularly are Boddington's Bitter and Castle Eden (the latter selling especially well) and a guest beer that may be Taylor Landlord.

To reach the final calling point, either return along Old Elvet, turn sharply left into New Elvet, and proceed until it becomes Hallgarth Street, or cut through Court Lane almost opposite the Dun Cow and turn left into New Elvet and ❦**The Victoria (8)**❦, a magnificent pub in all respects. While it is some distance from the town center, it is well worth making the brief extra journey. You'll find a bank of five relatively modern handpumps dispensing Theakston Best Bitter, Marston's Pedigree, Hodges Original from Crook in County Durham, and guest beers. The pub is completely unspoiled and features a distinctly triangular profile with separate rooms, wood floors, etched glass, a street corner door leading straight into the public bar, and many other novelties. It is, in fact, everything a traditional pub should be and certainly a member of a dying breed. Lunchtime food is available as well as overnight accommodation. This is the sort of place to linger, but not too long; you should allow approximately 20 minutes to return to the station.

15

EDINBURGH

Edinburgh is known as "the Athens of the North" because of the number of intellectuals, such as Boswell, Carlyle, and Scott, who lived there in the 18th and 19th centuries. It is the administrative and legal capital of Scotland and the seat of the new Scottish parliament. The contrast between the elegant and well laid out New Town and the mishmash and winding lanes of the Old Town is remarkable, but wherever you are in Edinburgh, there are good pubs to be found.

Start at the rear (southern) entrance to Waverley Station in Market Street, and directly opposite is Fleshmarket Close. Halfway up the stairs is the *Good Beer Guide* (CAMRA, 1999) listed ❚**Halfway House (1)**❚. It is tiny, friendly, noisy, often smoky, usually crowded, and well worth a visit. The beer range is constantly changing, but there are never fewer than four on sale. There is some interesting railway memorabilia.

Go down the steps and turn left into Market Street, then turn right to cross over Waverley Bridge. Turn right into Princes Street, cross it, and find West Register Street and the ❚**Guildford Arms (2)**❚. This is a classic Scottish Victorian gin palace with brewery mirrors, a minstrels gallery, screens, and a wonderful ceiling. It sells Belhaven 60/-, Caledonian Deuchars and 80/-, Orkney Dark Island, and up to six guest beers including at least one from Harviestoun. Lunch is available on weekdays.

"Edinburgh... lyric, brief, bright, clear and vital as a flash of lightning."

Charlotte Bronte

After leaving the Guildford, take a sharp left along the incongruously named Gabriel's Road (it's a footpath), keeping Register House, the original home of the world's first public land register, on your right. Carry on down West Register Street to St. Andrew Square. Turn right and follow the road all the way down the hill, where it becomes Dublin Street. If the weather is good there are great views across the River Forth to the sunny kingdom of Fife. At the bottom of the hill take the next left into Cumberland Street and the ❚**Cumberland Bar (3)**❚. This elegant, functional New Town pub has wood panelling, dark green leather seating, and a fine collection of brewery mirrors and framed posters. It won a CAMRA Pub Refurbishment Award. Beers on sale are Caledonian, Murray's Summer Ale, Deuchars

Top:
*Guildford
Arms*

Bottom:
Kay's Bar.

IPA and 80/-, and up to six guest ales all dispensed through tall fonts by air pressure. There is good food at lunchtime.

Turn left out of here and follow Cumberland Street for its full length to St. Vincent Street and the **St. Vincent Bar (4)**. This welcoming, traditional bar has a superb gantry and many interesting wall decorations. It sells Caledonian Deuchars IPA, Marston's Pedigree, and three guest beers and serves lunch during the week.

From here turn right, go up the hill, and turn right again into Jamaica Street. Go through the mews houses, and at the other side is **Kay's Bar (5)**. Cozy, comfortable, convivial, and consistent was the alliterative description in the *Good Beer Guide*. It sells Belhaven 80/- and beers from the Scottish Courage range along with 50 single malt whiskies and good value lunches.

From Jamaica Street turn left into India Street to Heriot Row. Turn right and then sharply left up Wemyss Place to Queen Street. Turn left along Queen Street and take the first right up Castle Street, which affords a marvelous view of Edinburgh Castle. Halfway up the hill you will find Young Street on your right and the unmissable **Oxford Bar (6)**, one of the few remaining unspoiled, turn-of-the-century pubs in Edinburgh. For many years it was run by the inimitable Willie Ross, who refused to serve — in no particular order — lager, women, and Englishmen! There is an ode to Willie on the wall as you enter the pub. It sells Belhaven IPA and 80/- and a basic range of food. Try the pies.

Thirty yards away on the left is the **Cambridge Bar (7)**. This bar dates from 1775 and is built in classic New Town

style. The wooden-floored interior has an eclectic collection of knickknacks. The regular beers are Caledonian Deuchars IPA and 80/-, Harviestoun Schiehallion, Marston's Pedigree, and an exciting range of guest beers. Good food is served at lunchtime. The pub is closed on Sunday.

Carry on along Young Street and turn left into North Charlotte Street. Pass George Street on your left and turn right along the southern boundary of Charlotte Square. Follow Hope Street until it becomes Queensferry Street, where you'll find ∎**H. P. Mathers (8)**∎, designed and built at the turn of the century. There are four tall founts dispensing Caledonian Deuchars IPA, Courage Directors, and two guest beers. Two handpumps dispense Theakston Best Bitter and a guest. Basic bar snacks are available all day. Admire the many old Scottish brewery mirrors on the walls, including a rare one from the Edinburgh United Brewery. (It was closed down and the head brewer and managing director were jailed after the Customs and Excise inspectors raided the brewery on Christmas day, 1934, and caught them brewing undeclared beer.)

Top: *Oxford Bar.*

Bottom: *Cambridge Bar*

You are now no more than one hundred yards from the fleshpots of Princes Street. If you are hungry, then it is worth knowing that Edinburgh has more restaurants per head than any other city in Britain.

16

EXETER

Exeter is a Roman town that was once a great port. It has a Maritime Museum with more than one hundred craft in the former docks. The cathedral has a three hundred-foot-long nave — the longest span of unbroken Gothic rib-vaulting in the world.

The crawl starts from St. David's Station. Cross the parking lot to the ❦**Great Western Hotel (1)**❦, a free house in a small independent, former railway hotel. It is comfortable and friendly with excellent beer and good value food. The bar manager is a real ale enthusiast, serving Draught Bass, Fuller's London Pride, and five or six beers mostly from independent breweries. Very popular with railway workers and the travelling public, it has overnight accommodation and is listed in the *Good Beer Guide* (CAMRA, 1999).

Cross the road to the ❦**Jolly Porter (2)**❦, a basic alehouse on several long and narrow levels. Another *Good Beer Guide* entry, it is very popular, especially with students, and keeps its beers well. Real ales include Courage Best, Courage Directors, John Smith Bitter, a Courage supplied guest beer, and a genuine independent guest beer. There is good value food daily and jazz on Wednesday evenings. The pub hosts a beer festival lasting two weeks in the autumn.

"The city of Exeter derives a very great correspondence with Holland, as also directly Portugal, Spain and Italy; shipping off vast quantities of woollen-manufactures…"

Daniel Defoe

Before heading up St. David's Hill, take a short detour to the bottom entrance of the ❦**Imperial (3)**❦, a vast Wetherspoon pub standing on its own grounds. Tastefully converted from a former hotel, it has three bars and conforms to the usual Wetherspoon policies of no music, a non-smoking area, food all day, and reasonably priced beers. A visit to the orangery is a must — it was designed by Isambard Kingdom Brunel. Regular beers on sale are Draught Bass, Courage Directors, Exmoor Stag, and two guest beers. Weston cider is sold in the orangery bar.

Leave the Imperial by the same way you went in and continue along St. David's Hill and over the Iron Bridge to the ❦**City Gate (4)**❦, which was recently renovated and reopened as a free house. In the main bar there is a very civilized atmosphere with quiet music; the cellar bar is livelier.

Above: *St. Anne's Well Brewery, home of the Fizgig & Firkin*

Draught Bass is a regular beer along with several changing guest offerings, often from local microbreweries. Food is available all day, and bed and break-fast will be available soon.

Cross the road and walk down the steps to the ❦Fizgig & Firkin (5)❦. It is a large, single-bar pub typical of the Firkin chain. The real ales are the usual Firkin range from its own brewery, including the ubiquitous Dogbolter and an occasional guest beer. It is housed on the ground floor of a former tower brewery, the St. Anne's Well Brewery, which owned 150 tied houses. Brewing ceased in 1967. This well setup pub has food all day, frequent live music, and facilities for the disabled.

Walk under the Iron Bridge down Exe Street. At the opposite end stands the ❦Mill-on-the-Exe (6)❦, a flagship pub for the St. Austell Brewery. It is large and smart with good views over the river from the terrace. A good range of St. Austell beers are sold: XXXX Mild, Tinners Ale, Trelawny's Pride, and HSD. It is open all day, and food is available most of the time. There are facilities for the disabled.

Leave by the front of the Mill-on-the-Exe, turn left, and continue along Bonhay Road back to the station.

HISTORIC GREENWICH

As one might expect in such a popular area for tourists, there are many pubs in and around Greenwich. The crawl visits the best and some of the most historic pubs in the area and takes in most of the sights. (The Millennium Dome is not covered, but it can be seen in the distance from the riverside pubs.)

A good start can be made from Greenwich BR and Docklands Light Railway Station at which buses 180 and 199 also stop. On leaving the station cross Greenwich High Road into Lang Place, then turn right, left, and right again for the **Ashburnham Arms (1)** in Ashburnham Grove. A *Good Beer Guide* (CAMRA, 1999) regular, this outstanding Shepherd Neame pub is well worth seeking out. On sale are Shepherd Neame Best Bitter, Masterbrew, Spitfire, and seasonal beers. It was named London CAMRA Pub of the Year in 1995 and has recently been extended to reflect its popularity. Excellent food is available at lunchtime — it was a recent winner of the brewery's Community Food Pub of the Year award. The beer garden is very popular during the summer.

Turn left on leaving and walk to the end of the road. Cross Greenwich South Street and follow Royal Hill as the road bends around. After the Prince Albert (Courage beers) you reach the **Richard I (2)**, which sells Young's Bitter, Special, and seasonal beers. This popular two-bar, bow-windowed pub was previously featured on CAMRA's national inventory of pub interiors. The pub was once owned by the Tolly Cobbold brewery of Ipswich and is still known locally as the Tolly House. It has a large beer garden featuring a barbecue area that is very popular in summer. It comes as a welcome relief from the hectic central pubs.

Continue to the end of Royal Hill and turn right into Greenwich High Road. A few yards along adjoining the Greenwich Cinema is the **Funnel and Firkin (3)**. This is a recent, welcome conversion by the Firkin Brewery of a pub that previously sold only keg beers. It now sells Firkin Shipshape, Funnel, Set's Ale, the ubiquitous Dogbolter, and seasonal beers supplied by the Flag and Firkin in Watford. It has the standard Firkin decor and innuendoes that will keep you amused.

Take a right turn and continue along Greenwich High Road towards the center. When you reach the one-way system, cross Nelson Road to enter the "central island." Go into the market through the alleyway running alongside Oddbins. At the far end of the market is the ❦**Admiral Hardy (4)**❦ in College Approach. This traditional one-bar pub is situated at the northern end of Greenwich market, close to all the tourist attractions. Interesting nautical memorabilia adorns the walls. It sells Shepherd Neame Best Bitter, Masterbrew, and guest beers.

From the front door turn left, cross College Approach, and turn right into Greenwich Church Street. About 25 yards along on the right is the ❦**Gipsy Moth (5)**❦, which sells Adnams Bitter, Tetley Bitter, and regular guest beers. It is a large, recently refurbished pub situated closer to the Cutty Sark than to Gipsy Moth IV. The pub was formerly known as the Wheatsheaf and was renamed and reopened by Sir Francis Chichester's widow in 1974. It is popular with tourists and local students.

Top: *Trafalgar Tavern.*

Bottom: *Cutty Sark.*

The easiest way to get to the next pub is to head towards the river and pass the Cutty Sark, the famous tea clipper now in dry dock. Follow the riverside path in front of the Royal Naval College and you will arrive at the ❦**Trafalgar Tavern (6)**❦ in Park Row. This large, multi-room pub is a listed building and was the *Evening Standard* Pub of the Year in 1995. The beer range has improved considerably in recent years thanks to the introduction of guest beers from independent regional breweries and microbreweries. On regular sale are Courage Best and Directors. Good quality food is served in a separate dining area open lunchtime and evenings. There is live jazz on Monday evenings.

Turn left upon leaving and take the first left into Crane Street. Follow the river past the rowing clubs and the power station until you arrive at the ❦**Cutty Sark (7)**❦ in Ballast Quay. This quayside, Georgian pub claims to have the only riverfront seating area in Greenwich. The nautical internal and external decor is interesting. Upstairs there is a large seating area where families are welcome at lunchtime. It sells Fuller's London Pride, Harvey Sussex Bitter, Morland Old Speckled Hen, and a guest beer.

On leaving here head back along the river until you get to Hoskins Street. Turn left and continue until the end of the road. Cross Trafalgar Road and start to go up Maze Hill, taking the first right into Park Vista, which, as the name suggests, runs along Greenwich Park, home to the National Maritime Museum. The Queen's House and Maritime Museum stand near the River Thames and alongside the famous baroque buildings of the Royal Naval College. These buildings are set against rolling parkland that sweeps uphill to the Old Royal Observatory from where all of London unfolds before the eye. The Royal Observatory has long since left London due to pollution.

On the right towards the end of the road is the ▮**Plume of Feathers (8)** ▮, our last stop. It is believed to be the only pub in Greenwich that actually lies on the Meridian. There has been a pub on the site since 1691. The current beer range — Morland Old Speckled Hen, Ruddle's Best, Webster Yorkshire Bitter, and Young's Special — may soon change. Excellent home-cooked food is available throughout the day. The pub has a walled garden and toys available for children.

About a five-minute walk away is Maze Hill BR station and buses 177, 180, 286, and 386.

MAP

18

HORSHAM

Horsham is a medium-sized town at the northern end of West Sussex, easily accessible from London by train. Probably the most significant feature of the town for most ale drinkers is the long-established King and Barnes brewery. But that is not the whole story.

Our crawl starts at Horsham station and involves about two miles of walking in total. From the station cross the footbridge from the main entrance and ticket office to the exit in Station Close. Immediately opposite the end of this road is our first stop, the ❦**Bedford Hotel (1)**❦, a large and welcoming street corner pub with two bars. The larger bar has two pool tables and a large screen TV that attracts locals for big sporting events. When things get busy, quiet can be found in the other bar. Take time to savor a pint of Fuller's London Pride, Morland Old Speckled Hen, or King and Barnes Sussex Bitter.

Top: The Bedford.

Bottom: The Tanner's Arms.

Leaving the Bedford, we take the longest part of the walk without any refreshment. Turn left along Station Road and left into Oakhill Road. Next turn right into Elm Grove, left into Bennett's Road, right at the T-junction into Compton's Lane, and right again into St. Leonard's Road. After a few yards you will come across the ❦**Forester's Arms (2)**❦ with its fenced front garden. It is one of Shepherd Neame's farthest flung outposts. This small, one-bar pub has a stone flagged floor, an open fire, original exposed beams, and hops draped over the bar. It is one of only a few pubs in Horsham where you can play a game of Sussex bar billiards while sipping your Masterbrew or Bishop's Finger.

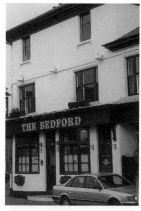

Suitably refreshed, leave the Forester's and continue along St. Leonard's Road to a T-junction. Ignoring the St. Leonard's Arms (no real ales available), turn right along Brighton Road. After a couple of hundred yards you come to the ❦**Tanner's Arms (3)**❦, the first King and Barnes tied house on this crawl. This is a small, roadside local with the emphasis on beer rather than food. There is a long public bar and a smaller lounge with a private room, or "snug." This pub keeps most of King and Barnes' beers, including Mild Ale.

On leaving the Tanner's, continue along Brighton Road. After a while you will pass by the **Queen's Head** *(4)* on the right, only worth a stop if you are very thirsty or completing the King and Barnes ale trail. Continue under the railway bridge, cross the miniroundabout into East Street, and come to the Tut 'n' Shive, a town center pub that is inexplicably popular with youngsters. Although it has a range of hand pumps, it is not unusual to see no real ales at all in this pub.

On arriving at the Market Square, you can turn left to find Bar Vin, one of an uninspiring chain of wine bars that sells Greenall and Tetley beers. Or far better, on the opposite side of the square, visit the ❦**Bear Inn (5)**❦. This compact King and Barnes town center hostelry has a range of reasonably priced food, but it gets very busy in the evenings. The Horsham Museum can be found just around the corner.

Turn left out of Market Square to continue along West Street to Shelley's Fountain, a work of art erected as part of the pedestrianization of this area of the town center to commemorate the author, Percy Bysshe Shelley, who lived nearby. At this corner, in premises formerly occupied by a pine shop, is a new Wetherspoon's pub named the **Lynd Cross** *(6)*. From here continue on past the **Green Dragon** *(7)*, a recently refurbished King and Barnes house, to the ❦**King and Barnes Brewery (8)**❦ itself. Tours are available during the week, although booking is advisable, and there is a brewery shop where one can buy King and Barnes ales, bottled beers, and souvenirs together with an interesting selection of wines. For those completing the King and Barnes trail there is another pub just beyond the brewery on the right in the Bishopric called the **King's Arms** *(9)*.

Turning left out of the brewery and left again into Albion Way, continue around the bend to the ❦**Malt Shovel (10)**❦ on the corner of Springfield Road. This pub is North Sussex

Top: *The Malt Shovel*.

Bottom: *Ye Old Stout House*.

CAMRA Branch's 1999 Pub of the Year and is part of the Hogshead chain. On entering the visitor is confronted with six handpumps and, just out of sight around the corner, three beers "on gravity." The enthusiastic landlord always gives a warm welcome to CAMRA members and keeps a continuously varied range of ales, all in excellent condition, as well as a selection of continental bottled beers. A month-long beer festival is held each spring.

After enjoying this hostelry, go directly across Albion Way and down the road opposite to return to the Shelley Fountain. Turn left into the pedestrianized West Street and left again at the junction with South Street to pass by the Crown (an uninspiring, noisy pub); bear right to arrive at ☙Ye Old Stout House (11)☙. This is a popular town center pub that concentrates on providing the full range of King and Barnes beers in excellent condition. This pub is closed from 4 P.M. until 7:30 P.M. each day and doesn't open at all on Tuesday evenings. A very limited range of snacks is available. It was refurbished a few years ago, losing its small backbar, but it retains an intimate atmosphere. It was deservedly voted Sussex CAMRA Pub of the Year and also won the Peter King Memorial Shield in 1997. From the Stout House, turn right and go up the steps directly ahead. Continue over the footbridge by the Sun Alliance building and straight along North Street to return to the station after a 10-minute walk.

19

HULL

Kingston upon Hull, to give the city its proper name, has a great maritime tradition and still remains one of Britain's major ports. Old docks have been converted into a modern, eye-catching marina, yet history is never far away. The Old Town with its wandering High Street is the base for our crawl. Pubs and museums combine to add interest to this crawl, and it also takes in three ornate, award-winning toilet blocks!

From the rail or bus station cross busy Ferensway, pass the Cenotaph, and proceed up Paragon Street. You will soon see the City Hall, where the Tourist Information Centre can be found on the corner of Queen Victoria Square. Ferens Art Gallery, the Town Docks Museum, and the first of the three toilet blocks are also situated on the square. Continue towards Whitefriargate, past the Princes Dock Shopping Centre, and turn right into the cobbled Princes Dock Street. The first turn on the left is Postengate, and here is our first pub, ❦**The Mission (1)**❦, the city's only Old Mill tied house.

Originally a seaman's mission, it reopened in 1995 after extensive internal alterations to a former club layout. The interesting interior includes the Old Chapel, refurbished to its former glory and complete with pulpit and stained-glass windows. This is the largest of the Old Town's pubs and is somewhat like a baronial hall together with its minstrel's gallery. It gets very busy on weekends. The full range of Old Mill beers is available and it offers a wide range of food Monday through Thursday until 3 P.M. and until 5 P.M. on Friday and Saturday. The pub has a Children's Certificate.

"Hull, though a sea-port, a place that I shall always look back to with delight."

William Cobbett

When you come out of the pub's main entrance, turn left down Dagger Lane and continue in a southerly direction to Castle Street (A63), an extremely busy street taking lorries and passengers to the docks and North Sea Ferries. Cross at the pedestrian crossing onto the site of the Hull Marina. Proceed down Humber Dock Street alongside the marina until you reach the River Humber. On the riverfront in Nelson Street is the ❦**Minerva Hotel (2)**❦.

The building dates from 1831 and, with displays of maps, charts and prints, it has a strong nautical feel. It has a central bar serving several different areas, including a former ladies' loo, possibly the smallest in the country, that now seats four people. Good food is available every lunchtime and from 6 P.M. until 9 P.M. Monday through Thursday. Accompanied children are welcome in the non-smoking area if taking meals. There are pleasant views across the Humber towards Lincolnshire on a fine day. Unfortunately, if you wish to use the outside drinking area, a local area bylaw insists on the use of plastic glasses. The pub sells Tetley Bitter, Taylor Landlord, and a regular guest beer (two in summer) often from Scottish breweries. Just across the road from the pub is the second of the ornate toilet blocks, catering to ladies and gentlemen.

Continue along the riverfront past the former Humber Ferry Terminal, and the junction of the Humber and Hull Rivers will be seen. We now follow the River Hull in a northerly direction up Queen Street. Turn right into Humber Street, and at the end is the Tidal Surge Barrier that is lowered when high tides threaten. Proceed up High Street under the Myton Bridge and the busy A63. (This route is easier than trying to cross at the junction of Queen Street and Castle Street, where there is no pedestrian crossing.) When you emerge from under the bridge take the signed footpath to the left, which will bring you out at the foot of the bridge. Then turn right into Market Place past the gilded statue of King Billy and the last of the three ornate toilet blocks — this one serves gentlemen only. Continue towards Holy Trinity, the largest parish church in England, which was founded in 1285 and retains much of its medieval brickwork.

Look for a large, blue bell hanging above the entrance to an alley on the left side of the road. This leads to one of Hull's most unspoiled pubs, ❦ **Ye Old Blue Bell (3)** ❦. It is owned by Samuel Smiths and sells Old Brewery Bitter and traditional food. The pub has three downstairs rooms, a drinking corridor, and an upstairs game room. It is closed on Sunday afternoons. The entrance alley actually continues through an outdoor drinking area into Hull's covered market.

Returning up the alley to Market Place, continue left for a few yards before turning left into Silver Street. Not far down on the right side, look for the hanging sign of the next pub, ❦ Ye Olde White Harte (4) ❦, another pub accessible only from an alley. It is probably one of the oldest buildings in the city and was once the home of Hull's military governors. This Grade II listed building is famous for its upstairs "Plotting Parlour," where in 1642, according to local folklore, Sir John Hotham decided to bar Charles I from the town, an act said to have triggered the Civil War. It has two downstairs bars, each of which features sit-in fireplaces, on either side of the dark wooden staircase. There are two upstairs dining rooms and an outside drinking area. Beers featured are Courage Directors, McEwan 80/-, Theakston XB and Old Peculier, and an occasional guest.

Below: Ye Olde Black Boy.

Retrace your steps up Silver Street and cross Market Place straight into Scale Lane. The last building on the right, now a tearoom, is the oldest domestic building in the city. Turn left back into the medieval High Street, and just around the corner is ❦ Ye Olde Black Boy (5) ❦, now owned by Enterprise Inns. It retains a bar, a wood-panelled front room where the pub's history is displayed, and two upstairs rooms. On sale are eight constantly changing real ales, real cider, and foreign bottled beers including draught Hoegaarden wheat beer from Belgium.

Continue up High Street, and on the right are three of Hull's museums. First is the Hull and East Riding Museum, then the Street Life Museum, and finally Wilberforce House, the birthplace of the famous anti-slavery campaigner William Wilberforce. Continue until you reach the junction with Alfred

Gelder Street. You may now wish to leave the main route to include another pub on the crawl that is worthy of a visit because it is the only tied house of the present Hull Brewery.

EXTRA PUB ROUTE: Cross Drypool Bridge to your right and go straight across at the traffic light junction with Great Union Street into Clarence Street. *The Red Lion (6)* is only four hundred yards from Drypool Bridge and was built for local brewers Moors and Robson in 1939. With a shop-front bar in the main room, it has all the style of a '30s pub. Hull Brewery Bitter and an occasional guest beer are available. You are now at the furthest point from the rail and bus stations; if short of time, you may now wish to catch one of the many buses that stops on the same side of the road as the pub. To rejoin the main route of the crawl, return to the crossroads and turn right down Great Union Street. At the main road junction with Witham, turn left and cross North Bridge to return to the west side of the River Hull with Wincolmlee to your right.

STAYING ON THE MAIN ROUTE: Cross Alfred Gelder Street and continue along the western bank of the River Hull via Dock Office Row. When you reach the main road you will see North Bridge to the right and Wincolmlee straight ahead.

Whatever your decision, you should now head along Wincolmlee where you will find the ♛**Bay Horse Hotel (7)**♛ situated four hundred yards down on the corner of Mitchell Street. This small, cozy, street corner local has a small bar full of Rugby League memorabilia and a spectacular, lofty stable lounge. Good value, home-cooked food includes teatime special offers and Sunday lunches. Most of the range of Bateman's beers from Lincolnshire are on offer.

The rail and bus stations are some 20 minutes away at a steady walk. There are a number of return routes, and one of the quickest allows you to take in another decent pub if you wish. Return down Wincolmlee, turn right into New George Street, and continue across into Francis Street. Turn left at the crossroads and head down Charles Street. Cross the main road (Freetown Way), which splits the street into two.

On the corner of John Street is the **New Clarence (8)**. Built across the road from the original Clarence, this is a Tetley Festival Alehouse that is a very reasonable conversion from a co-op store. It sells Tetley Dark Mild and Bitter, Marston's Pedigree, and a good selection of guest ales and bottled beers from Belgium. Food is available at lunchtime and on early weekday evenings. You're now only 10 minutes from both stations, and you are advised to use Bond Street and Jameson Street as the quickest route back.

20

HYDE ROAD, MANCHESTER

Hyde Road is quite historic. It was built by the Manchester, Hyde, and Mottram Turnpike Trust through fields between Ardwick and Hyde. Work commenced in 1819 with toll bars at Canal Bridge in Denton and Devonshire Street near Ardwick Station. Later a number of side bars were opened, including one at the Plough.

This is a linear crawl of about one and half miles, starting about two miles from the center of Manchester, through the suburb of Gorton along the A57 towards Hyde. The road eventually goes to Glossop and over the High Peak to Sheffield.

Several buses (numbers 200, 201, 203, 204 and 207) run along the entire length of the crawl approximately every 10 minutes from Piccadilly Gardens in the city center. Alight at the Pottery Lane stop. An hourly train service (two hourly on Sunday) runs from Piccadilly station to Marple, stopping at Belle Vue station, which is partway along the crawl, as the maps shows.

The first and appropriately named stop is the ♥ **Travellers' Call (1)** ♥ on Hyde Road at its junction with Pottery Lane (A5184). This is a Hyde's pub with a taproom in the good, old-fashioned Manchester basic style. It is a robust boozer that can be noisy, particularly on football nights, but it is always friendly and has an atmosphere to be cherished. It is open all day. The nearby *Nag's Head* sells Burtonwood beers and might be worth a call if you have time.

Move along the north side of the road about a quarter of a mile to the ♥ **Coach and Horses (2)** ♥, which is actually in Belle Vue Street (A6010) at its junction with Hyde Road. A regular describes it as the "quintessential local with the quintessential pint of Robbies." It is a gem that is family run and firmly part of the community. Robinson's cask beers far outsell all other drinks. There is a television in the vault — popular for sport — but otherwise the only sounds are those of

conversation. It is not only popular with locals but also with cinemagoers from the Showcase opposite and the nearby Belle Vue speedway track. It is open all day on weekends but only from 5:30 P.M. during the week.

A little further along on the opposite side of the road is Belle Vue railway station. Set back from the road on the north side is the *Pineapple (3)*, another Hyde's pub selling the budget priced Billy Westwood's Bitter. There is also a good collection of photographs of the fondly remembered Belle Vue Zoo and Amusement Park. Stay with the north side for the ▪**Suburban (4)**▪, a John Willy Lees street corner pub now on an island site and part of a rebuilt town center. It has a comfortable lounge and a basic vault with some fine prints of 19th-century Gorton. There is also a "Morris Room" used by the local Gorton Morris Men, who take an active part in the annual Rushcart procession in mid-September. The pub has a fine collection of cartoons.

Next comes the ▪**Plough (5)**▪, another gem owned by Robinson's. It is listed as a building of architectural and historic interest, which no doubt helped to save it from a threat of demolition for road widening. A local says the vault "is a symphony in wood." Note the beautiful tiles.

A little further along is the Lord Nelson, mentioned merely as a landmark. Just after this pub is a footpath that leads to the otherwise hidden ▪**Vale Cottage (6)**▪, which sells beers from Scottish Courage's extensive list as well as guest ales. This is a country pub completely different from the others on the crawl. It has a relaxed atmosphere, and with high standards and excellent lunches, it is well worth the slight detour. There are evening meals until 7:30 P.M.

Cross the road and note the Brookfield Unitarian Church, which dates from 1871 and has a tower housing eight bells. It replaced the old Dissenting Chapel built in 1703.

Close by is the ▌Waggon and Horses (7)▌, a Holt's pub with the tradition of fine beers at low prices. It has been sensibly modernized with four distinct areas: a vault, a games area, a main lounge, and a "back room." It is justifiably popular and, apart from live entertainment on Saturday evenings, it is yet another temple of conversation and drinking. It is open all day.

Our final stop is two hundred yards along Hyde Road to the ▌Friendship (8)▌, owned by Marston's but selling Bateman's Mild. This is a well named pub with sing-along style entertainment on weekends and four separate rooms if you include the lobby. The vault is particularly characterful. The pub closes in the afternoon during the week.

21

KENDAL

Kendal, often known as the "Auld Grey Town," is a picturesque market town in attractive surroundings only a mile or two outside the Lake District National Park. It is built of local stone and has many old yards and alleys, often identified by numbers. There are two particularly interesting buildings: the amazingly spacious parish church at the south end of the town and the castle that stands on a mound a little to the east. The view of the Lakeland mountains from the castle is truly spectacular.

Kendal is well served by public transport. It is on a branch line from Oxenholme on the main west coast railway line with some fast trains from Manchester Airport. The Ribble Bus Company runs a stagecoach service (No. 555) from Lancaster to Keswick that stops at Kendal.

An appropriate starting point is at either the railway or bus station. Turn right out of the first or left out of the other into Sandes Avenue, and at the end on the right in Stricklandgate is the ▮**Sawyer's Arms (1)**▮. This is a pub from the former Hartley's brewery of Ulverston, now owned by Robinson of Stockport. It sells Best Bitter and Hartley XB. Hot lunches are served and there are evening meals in summer. There is also bed and breakfast accommodation. This is a characterful, three-storey pub with an attractive frontage and some well preserved, etched Hartley's windows.

Carry on along Stricklandgate towards the town center, turning left into the bustling Market Place. The easily located ▮**Globe Inn (2)**▮, Thwaites's only tied house in Kendal, was recently modernized. Thwaites Bitter and the stronger Golden Charmer are on sale along with good value food at lunchtime.

Proceed further down Stricklandgate to where it becomes Highgate, near the handsome Town Hall with its clock tower. Look carefully on the right for a sign stating simply "Yard 2." The ▮**White Hart Hotel (3)**▮ is in an exceedingly quaint alley, yet the pub itself is very modern. Like the Sawyer's Arms, it has fine Hartley's windows. This is another Robinson

Above: *The Ring O'Bells.*

pub selling Best Bitter and Hartley XB. Meals are served at lunchtime, when families are welcome, but there is no food on Sunday. It provides accommodation.

It is a bit of a climb to the next pub, but well worth it. Go up All Hallows Lane to the ▮**Black Swan (4)**▮. It dates back to 1764 and is one of the few basic and unaltered pubs in the area. There are two rooms, no jukebox or game machines, real fires, a great welcome, and loads of atmosphere. Theakston Best Bitter is the only regular beer, but there are guest ales in summer. Lunchtime food is available on Sunday and every day in summertime. There is accommodation.

Backtrack a little to the ▮**Cask House (5)**▮, a back-to-basics town center pub with wooden floors. There are usually three regular beers on sale — Boddington's Bitter, Marston's Pedigree, and Wadworth 6X — together with a traditional cider and guest beers in summer. Meals are served up to 7:30 P.M.

Return to Highgate and cross it, taking note of Beers in Particular, an off-license pub where a great selection of bottled beers is sold, including many from abroad. Draught beers, usually from Dent Brewery, can be taken away in containers. Move on to the ▮**Ring O'Bells (6)**▮, which is actually situated within the parish church graveyard and is on consecrated land. Beers sold are Lorimer's Best Scotch, Vaux Bitter and Samson, Wards Best Bitter, and a guest ale. This lovely little pub can hardly have changed during the present century. It has tiny rooms, an interesting assortment of miscellaneous chairs and tables, and a welcoming coal fire. Don't miss the tiny private room, or "snug," with its unusual coffin table, found between the two bars. It is on CAMRA's list of historic pub interiors. The pub closes during the afternoon, but food is available during both sessions. Bed and breakfast accommodation is available.

Cross Highgate again and return towards the town center for the ▮**Brewery Arts Centre (7)**▮. It stands on rising ground and is clearly marked from Highgate. This was the former

Whitwell Mark Brewery, which ceased brewing in 1968. There is plenty going on here, so finding the bar may be a problem, but do persist. The beers are from the Vaux and Wards range together with a guest. There are also some splendid catering facilities here with much imagination shown in the choice of menu.

Above: *Bridge Hotel.*

You are now faced with a longish walk — 10 to 12 minutes — along Highgate. Turn right into Finkle Street. This is the heart of old Kendal, and there is much wonderful, ancient property to be seen. The street name changes to Stramondgate, and just before the broad, normally shallow River Kent is reached, the ❦**Bridge Hotel (8)**❦ is seen straight ahead. This pub has atmosphere as well as consistently good beer, although the choice may be restricted to Boddington's Bitter and Marston's Pedigree. The rooms are small, well maintained, and intimate, and there is a large and welcoming coal and log fire. Catering is a prominent feature, but this is essentially a pub with a public bar and eating facilities rather than a restaurant that also serves drinks. Accommodation is available.

Carry on along the same road, crossing the river towards the station, and turn right into Castle Street. The long, low, stone-built ❦**Castle Inn (9)**❦ is your final stop. This is a most successful pub selling Tetley Bitter, Theakston Best Bitter, several guest ales, and a house beer Castle Gate, a medium-strength bitter brewed by the Cartmel Brewery in Kendal. Food served at lunchtime is extremely good value, and the range and quality are remarkable. Note the framed windows from the former Dutton brewery. There is bed and breakfast accommodation.

Allow yourself a few extra minutes to return to the stations. They are not far away, but there is a busy road to cross and a final slope up to the railway station.

22

KINGTON

Kington is a small Herefordshire market town close to the Welsh border. It is famous for magnificent displays of 30-foot-high rhododendrons in spring and its sheep sales in autumn. It stands on the A44, which runs from Worcester, Bromyard, and Leominster through Kington into Wales, close to Llandrindod Wells, and eventually to Aberystwyth.

Start at the ❦**Queen's Head (1)**❦ in Bridge Street (A44). The pub has a functional public bar with wooden floorboards where traditional pub games, notably quoits and darts, coexist with gaming machines and a jukebox. The beer range consists of Dunn Plowman Brewhouse Bitter, brewed on the premises; Hobson Best Bitter; and S.P. Sporting Ales Double Top. Lunch is served in the lounge bar, at present only on Friday, Saturday, and Sunday. The exposed beams and comfortable seats and tables provide an attractive setting in which to eat. Pizzas are a speciality.

Top: Queen's Head.

Bottom: Ye Olde Tavern.

Next door to the Queen's Head is *The Talbot (2)*, an undistinguished, one-bar pub popular with younger drinkers, but offering only a basic Scottish Courage range.

Turn right from Bridge Street into Victoria Road, walking past some old black and white cottages on the right. After about five minutes you come to a row of Victorian brick, terraced houses at the eastern edge of the town. Among them is ❦**Ye Olde Tavern (3)**❦. This absolute gem was joint winner of Herefordshire CAMRA's Pub of the Year Award in 1993 (it then went on to win the area award for that year) and was runner-up in 1997 (losing by only one vote!).

Above: *The Old Fogey.*

Ansell Bitter is the only beer sold through a lovely old beer engine that prevents the brew from having a bit of a foaming head. There are two bars with settles and benches that are packed with curios. The pub is on CAMRA's register of pubs with outstanding interiors.

Retrace your steps, and instead of turning left back into Bridge Street, continue straight on into High Street. On the left nestling amongst the shops is ▮**The Old Fogey (4)**▮, a warm and welcoming basic, one-bar pub with an unspoiled interior. It serves a variety of beers from independent breweries, including Hobson Best Bitter, Wood Special, and Fuller's London Pride. There is a patio drinking area at the back of the pub.

Continuing along High Street you come to the Market Hall, which, unusual for this area, is a red brick structure with an imposing clock tower. Take the right fork into Church Street and come to the ▮**Swan Hotel (5)**▮ on the right. This is mainly food-oriented with a good restaurant. The lounge bar in which Ansell Bitter is sold includes an original stone fireplace dating from when the pub was built in the 17th century. Accommodation is available here.

At this stage you might consider walking a further one hundred yards along Church Street to satisfy the curiosity of visiting "the last pub in England" — the Welsh border is just up the road! *The Royal Oak (6)*, also known as "the first and last," has a rather plain public bar at the front with a real fire and a comfortable lounge at the back. Beers vary, but they are usually somewhat mundane and expensive offerings.

23

LANCASTER

The name of Lancashire's first city comes from being a Roman camp (castrum) on the River Lune, although the city has prehistoric origins. John of Gaunt was the first Duke of Lancaster and ancestor of the royal house. For centuries it was an important port much involved in the slave trade. The castle dominates the city and houses law courts and a prison.

Start with three pubs on St. George's Quay on the south bank of the River Lune at the north end of the city. The ❦**Wagon and Horses (1)**❦ — a small, traditional pub with a decor of Irish football and rugby shirts, scarves, and photos — is the perfect place to start a crawl. There is a choice of three traditional beers from Robinson's, including Hartley XB, which recognizes a former owner. There is a small menu of homemade food served during lunchtime and in the evenings. Live music on Saturday evenings and bed and breakfast accommodation is available year-round. This pub affords great riverside views.

Head back towards the city center and call in at the ❦**George and Dragon (2)**❦. This small, pleasant pub has some excellent windows from the former Yates Castle Brewery of Ardwick, Manchester. It sells Wards Best Bitter and Thorne Best Bitter and also a guest beer.

"Lancaster... locked in between the hills on one side high as the clouds, and the sea on the other..."

Daniel Defoe

A little further along is the ❦**Three Mariners (3)**❦, which was formerly known as the Carpenter's Arms. Its handsome, large facade is covered by ivy and makes a pleasing contrast to the factories that surround it. This is said to be Lancaster's oldest pub, dating back to the 13th century. Ask to see the cellar — it's upstairs! Mitchell's beers are on sale, including the seasonal specials.

Carefully cross the busy highway (A6), and behind the bus station is ❦**The Bobbin (4)**❦, originally called the Priory. This large, bright, modern pub was completely refurbished in 1997. It serves Mitchell's draught beers, including Mitchell's Original Bitter and the renowned Lancaster Bomber. A variety of hot and cold snacks are available all day, and there is a pool table in the middle of the bar. There is live music on Thursday and big band jazz on the first Sunday of each month.

Head southeast to the ❦**Friary and Firkin (5)**❦, which was a church before opening as a pub in the spring of 1997. The renovations have not changed the inside of the building a great deal. One can still climb the steps and sit in the upper level with a view of the whole bar. Beers served include Tuck's Tipple and the Firkin brewery favorite, Dogbolter. This is not a brewpub; the beers are from another Firkin pub. Some of the main attractions of this large pub/monastery are the draughts and the giant games such as Jenga and Connect 4, which stand about four feet high.

Top: *The Three Mariners.*

Bottom: *The Water Witch.*

❦**The Penny Bank (6)**❦ is in Penny Street, which runs parallel to and between the two main roads of Lancaster. It is another pub that has taken its name from the building's original use. It opened in 1996 following its conversion from a Natwest Bank. An array of regular beers including Boddington's, Castle Eden, and Marston's Pedigree are served together with a selection of guest beers that changes every week. There is a rather daft practice here called the "gallon challenge." Find out about it, but do not be tempted to take part.

At the south end of the town is ❦**The Water Witch (7)**❦, a canal-side pub and one of the most popular pubs in Lancaster, especially during the summer, when the beer garden rapidly fills up. There are two floors inside the pub and a long bar offering rapid service. Boddington's and John Smith are the main beers along with Witches' Water, the house beer. Food is served during lunch hours, with the second floor converting into a restaurant during the evening. There is live music on weekends. The annual Lancaster Canal Festival in June draws many boat owners to the towpath garden.

Turn back towards the town center, and on the station approach is ❦**The Merchants (8)**❦, another claimant to be the oldest pub in Lancaster. It has been in business since 1668. This lively pub is next to the prison, and the entire pub is situated in the old sewer system of Lancaster. There are three main drinking areas, long rooms with tables on each side, and a spacious beer garden ideal for groups. Most of Theakston's beers are served with good food available all day. This pub gets very busy during the weekend.

Move back into Market Street and the precinct for the ♥**John O'Gaunt (9)**♥, a small city center pub with a splendid original frontage. The pub still retains traditional hours (i.e. it closes between 3 P.M. and 6 P.M.). This is a great place for jazz, with music most evenings and every Sunday lunchtime. Jim Bullseye Bowen is often in and gives guest performances on the trumpet. The atmosphere is lively and there is a good choice of beers: Tetley Bitter, Draught Burton Ale, Jennings Bitter, Boddington's, and guests. Families are made very welcome when taking meals.

24

LEDBURY *close just north*

Ledbury is an unspoiled market town in Hereford's hop-growing country overlooked by the Malvern Hills. The 17th-century Market House standing on oak pillars is the town's most outstanding building. Poet Laureate John Masefield was born here. The pubs reflect the historic nature of the town.

The six pubs in this crawl are all very close together —indeed the furthest away and the most southerly, the Royal Oak in the Southend, is only a 15-minute walk from Ledbury Railway Station, which is at the far north end of the town and served by direct trains from Hereford, Worcester, Birmingham, and London (Paddington). Three of the pubs offer accommodation and are ideal places to stay to explore this idyllic part of England.

The railway station is a good place to start the crawl. Walk up the Homend to the ❦**Horseshoe Inn (1)**❦ on the left. Enter this black and white building up a short flight of stairs into a single-bar pub. It is owned by the Hereford-based Rustic Pub Company and serves a variety of ales, mainly from independent breweries, such as Hobson Best Bitter and Wood Shropshire Lad. Food is served all day. Despite 20th-century refurbishment and trappings, it still retains some characterful elements such as exposed beams and cozy alcoves. There is a small outdoor drinking area.

"...fair and half-timbered houses black and white."

John Masefield

Turn left out of the Horseshoe and head south down the Homend into High Street to view the impressive black and white building on oaken stilts. This is the 17th-century Market Hall; from here turn left into Church Lane, a narrow cobbled street that has changed little since the middle ages. In this delightful setting is the ❦**Prince of Wales (2)**❦, a cozy, welcoming little gem dating from the 16th century. It appears on the lid of many a chocolate box and serves Banks' and Hanson's beers and Weston cider during the summer. Food is served at lunchtime throughout the year, and there are evening meals Friday through Sunday in the summer months. There are two main bar areas mixing comfort and character, and there is live folk music on Wednesday.

Retrace your steps back to High Street and cross over by the public library. Then head down Bye Street, past the cattle market and fire station, and on the right in a narrow back street is the ▮**Brewery Inn (3)**▮, a redbrick structure owned by Marston's but also selling Banks' Mild and a traditional cider. The private room, or "snug," which is full of character, was not touched during a recent refurbishment and is said to have the smallest bar in Herefordshire. There is also a game room on the first floor. Sandwiches and snacks are served at lunchtime except on Sunday.

Return along Bye Street, turning right into the High Street past the Feathers Hotel, which will be visited later. Continue straight on at the crossroads into the Southend to the ▮**Royal Oak Hotel (4)**▮. This pub shares a base with the Ledbury Brewery in the original brewhouse that was closed for 75 years but reopened in 1996. The main bar is food-oriented, but a smaller downstairs public bar is more for drinkers. Meals are served at lunchtime and in the evenings. Beers are from the attached brewery and are usually from single varietal hop strains: Ledbury Challenger SB and Northdown Winter are examples, and there are also seasonal offerings. Overnight accommodation is available.

Top: *Prince of Wales.*

Bottom: *Royal Oak.*

Retrace your steps along the Southend and turn left into New Street to the *Ye Olde Talbot (5)*, another black-and-white-fronted pub, which dates back to 1596 and was formerly a coaching inn. It sells beers from the Carlsberg Tetley stable. It also has a restaurant and provides overnight accommodation.

Finally, heading back along New Street, turn left at the crossroads into High Street and head to the ▮**Feathers Hotel (6)** ▮, an imposing black and white structure close to the Market Hall. Draught Bass, Worthington Bitter, and Fuller's London Pride are the cask beers on sale here. It has a restaurant and there are bedrooms to let. A beer festival is held here on August bank holiday weekend as part of the Ledbury Carnival; its procession takes place on the Monday.

Top: *Feathers Hotel.*

Bottom: *Market Hall.*

MAP

25

LEEDS TO MANCHESTER AND BACK BY RAIL

Here is a crawl that's a bit different. It calls for very little walking — from the train to the bar and from the bar to the train! You can suit yourself and do this crawl the other way around if you wish, or even join it partway through. The advantage of starting from Leeds is that you are on the correct platform at the first two stops. There are two routes to Manchester from Leeds, so make sure you use the Huddersfield line. Otherwise, if you go via Halifax and Rochdale, you will miss all the interesting bits (and privatized railway tea is no better than it was in the days of British Rail). A sound bit of advice is to pick up a copy of the Metro Train timetable at the Gateway Yorkshire tourist information office by the station entrance.

Above: Coopers.

If you start after 11A.M., make your first stop at ▮Coopers (1)▮, which is just inside the concourse of Leeds City Station. This is the former refreshment rooms and now operates as a bar with all the amenities that were previously there: coffee, tea, soft drinks, snacks, and hot meals. Three cask beers are sold, with John Smith Bitter and Draught Bass as regulars, and a guest beer. There are also some interesting bottled beers amongst the dross such as Hoegaarden and Staropramen. All the beers are pricey, so if you have the time and are not simply following this pub crawl, you would be better off crossing the road to the Scarbrough, a Festival Alehouse offering better value and choice. However, the food at the Coopers is reasonably priced, and the large room is comfortable and well appointed with plenty of indications of the coopers' trade.

There are three trains each hour to the first stop, which is Dewsbury. Just be careful not to catch an express to Liverpool (usually at eight minutes past the hour), for these trains do not

Top: *The West Riding.*

Bottom: *Head of Steam.*

stop at Dewsbury. Here is the ❦**West Riding Refreshment Rooms (2)**❦, which you can enter directly from the platform. There is a range of Black Sheep beers and several guests, mainly from local breweries, including one beer from the Linfit brewery. There is a main bar with a dining room to one side and a smaller room to the other with its own hatch. Food is well prepared and reasonably priced, and a great favorite is the curry night on Wednesday. The music is good, both recorded and live, and there are frequent festivals. As one might expect, there is a fair amount of railway memorabilia and a collection of pictures of Dewsbury pubs in older times. Check your train times, although every westbound train from here stops at Huddersfield.

The Huddersfield refreshment room is the ❦**Head of Steam (3)**❦, one of a group that includes pubs at Euston station in London and Newcastle. It was formerly the ticket office and waiting room of the Lancashire and Yorkshire Railway, the junior partner to the London and North Western Railway in the ownership of the impressive, classical style Huddersfield Railway Station. Black Sheep Bitter, a Bass beer, along with two local beers and three guests are on sale together with a variety of bottled beers. There are regular themed beer festivals. Beers at Head of Steam are not cheap, but they are interesting and kept in excellent condition. The food is also superb and is reasonably priced. There is live music — blues, jazz, folk — Sunday through Thursday evenings and a jazz brunch at Sunday lunchtime.

If you take a stopping train to Manchester you could drop off at Marsden, where the Burtonwood beers at the ❦**Station Hotel (4)**❦ are usually in excellent form, and at the ❦**Station (5)**❦ at Ashton-under-Lyne for a great choice of beers from independent breweries. However, the service through these stations is hourly and takes you to Manchester Victoria station, where the ❦Station Bar (6)❦ serves rather expensive Draught Bass and Boddington's Bitter. But it is worth visiting to see the amazing decorated glass globe, marble pillars, and carved wood, which are happy memories of the days of real railways. From Victoria catch the Metrolink tram to Piccadilly, which is where you would have arrived if you had taken a fast train from Huddersfield. Incidentally, whichever way you travel, do not be tempted to alight at Stalybridge. Save this delight for the return journey!

From the Metrolink Station take the ground-level exit to London Road, and opposite is ❦Munroe's (7)❦, a tribute to the much loved Marilyn. There are photographs and models of her all over this very comfortable pub with a split-level lounge and a smaller dining room. Boddington's Bitter and Flowers IPA are on sale at what might be termed mid-Manchester prices. There is a bistro during lunch hours.

From here return to the main-line station and take a Leeds train, making sure it stops at Stalybridge. You will be on the correct platform for the ❦Station Buffet (8)❦. Although it is not the only buffet bar of this sort, it is the best known. It has remained unchanged since 1885, except for a recent refurbishment that now allows the pub to boast two bars with a room linking them. On regular sale are Wadworth 6X and Flowers IPA along with up to six guest beers and a traditional cider. Bar snacks are available, including the famous black

Below: *Station Buffet.*

peas. Saturday is folk night, and there are periodic beer festivals. (For more information see the pub crawl of Stalybridge beginning on page 151).

You are on the right platform to return to Leeds. It's been a long day, so have a nap or a cup of tea. There is always Coopers at the other end.

26

LEE VALLEY BY BOAT

Good Beer Guide Editor Roger Protz once wrote, "there can be no better way to see the rural delights and industrial heritage of Britain than along the country's canals and rivers." So here is an opportunity. Much of the detail is from *The Best Waterside Pubs* by Chris Rowland and John Simpson.

This out-of-the-ordinary pub crawl along the River Lee starts in suburban London and finishes 25 miles out in rural Hertfordshire. That is, of course, unless you choose to travel in the opposite, southbound, direction. It will take you as long as you like, depending on how many stops you make and whether you decide to stay overnight. Sadly, only one of the recommended pubs provides bed and breakfast. You could walk the towpath, but it is quite a long way between pubs.

Top: *Princess of Wales.*

Bottom: *Anchor and Hope.*

The starting point is at the first pub, ❦**The Princess of Wales (1)**❦, at Lee Bridge on Lee Bridge Road, London E5. The nearest railway station is Clapton on the Liverpool Street line to Chingford. There are plenty of buses, and parking is available at the pub. Up until December 1997 this pub was called The Prince of Wales, but the name was changed in memory of Diana, Princess of Wales, who was a personal friend of John Young, Chairman of Young's Brewery. As one would expect, it sells Young's Bitter, Special, and the brewery's seasonal ales. There are three bars all finely panelled and well furnished, one of which is a separate restaurant. There is a good selection of food, including a seafood stall on the riverside. It is a popular pub with boaters and anglers.

Cast off for a short run by the Walthamstow Marshes to the ❦**Anchor and Hope (2)**❦, an East London institution in Upper Clapton. This small, one-bar pub is approved of by residents and visitors alike. Fuller's London Pride and ESB are on sale. Finding it by road is very difficult, but it is completely worthwhile to locate this gem.

Go along under Horse Shoe Bridge, past a series of reservoirs, stopping if you wish at the ***Narrow Boat (3)*** at Tottenham Hale. This pub may or may not have real ale on sale. There are three handpumps, but they are not always dispensing beer. It's better to move on to the ❦**Watersedge (4)**❦, half a mile to the north at Stonebridge Lock. With the obvious intention of serving users of the waterways, this former cafe has been successfully converted into a small pub that sells the full range of Fuller's beers.

It is a long run alongside innumerable reservoirs, sports clubs, housing estates, and industrial buildings — all the trappings of suburbia — to Enfield Lock and the ❦**Greyhound (5)**❦. It is on the east bank, across the road from the lock. McMullen Original AK and Country Best Bitter are the beers on sale, and lunch is available on weekdays. Nearby is the former Royal Ordnance small arms factory, where the famous Lee Enfield 303 rifle was manufactured. The Greyhound is a straightforward boozer probably built during the Great War. The pubs at Enfield Lock, like Carlisle, were part of the State Management Scheme — in effect nationalisation, but in reality an attempt to keep munitions workers sober to help the war effort. It is a welcoming pub with a dart board and linoleum in the public bar and comfy chairs and carpet in the lounge. In summer there is a pleasant terrace by the water.

It is a short trip to the ❦**Old English Gentleman (6)**❦ at Waltham Abbey, a fine old pub. This McMullen's pub sells Original AK and Country Best Bitter. Though modest in scale, it is a delightfully situated architectural jewel. The building is L-shaped and has a splendid tiled roof with decorative barge-boarded gable ends. A large vine, growing on trellis work supported by rustic beams, shades the little towpath-level beer garden, giving it a continental feel. Inside there are two small, low-ceilinged roofs, plenty of

Below: *Old English Gentleman.*

interesting objects on the walls, high stools at the bar, and a good pubby atmosphere. Sandwiches and rolls are sold at lunchtime. It is a good pub to stop at to recognize the changes from urban north London to rural home counties.

It's now time for a pleasant, leisurely, and relaxing run through the fields and meadows of Hertfordshire. At Hoddesdon the River Stort branches off on its journey to Bishop's Stortford. But your journey goes through a series of pretty villages to Ware and the ❦**Victoria (7)**❦, which stands 250 yards north of the town bridge. Only McMullen Original AK is sold, and meals are served at lunchtime. History abounds here; the building probably dates back to the 17th century or even earlier. The name gives us an idea as to how long it has been a public house. The red-brick rear of the pub is Georgian and overlooks a spacious terrace and patrons-only moorings. There are two bars with separate entrances — a taproom where darts holds sway and an attractive, interesting saloon with lots of plates and bric-à-brac on the walls.

The last stretch winds its pleasant way though willow-lined meadows to the county town of Hertford. (The river's navigational limit is in the town center.) By the fine old Mill Bridge is the ❦**Old Barge (8)**❦. There is a good range of beers including Adnams Bitter, Green King Abbot Ale, Ind Coope Burton Ale, Tetley Bitter, Young's Special Bitter, and Benskins Best Bitter, plenty to reflect on after a journey well travelled. There are some excellent views from the pub's terrace: you can see the bridge, a 17th-century mansion, and the tower of McMullen's brewery. The pub lies side-on to the river, and the main building has a discreet, orange brick Victorian frontage

Below: The Old Barge.

with an attractive doorway flanked by two bay windows. Inside you will find a cheerful atmosphere with open fireplaces, high-backed settles, exposed beams, and a variety of drinking and dining areas. Food is important here, and the pub is a popular lunchtime venue, particularly in summer.

27

LINCOLN

Both the main bus and railway stations are at the bottom of the town, close to the River Witham. It is a steep climb to the historic part of the city, but buses run from both places. If a car is used, start from the Westgate parking lot just below the walls of the castle and opposite the Toy Museum.

Head along Eastgate to the most distant of the chosen pubs, the ❚**Morning Star (1)**❚ on Greetwell Gate. There is a cheery welcome here and a choice of Theakston XB, Draught Bass, Ruddle Best, Wells Bombardier, and also a guest beer. Meals are served at lunchtime. A display of drawings, paintings, and photographs of aircraft reflect the landlord's career in the Royal Air Force and with British Aerospace. It is a comfortable pub with two interlinked front rooms where the only noise is conversation. The landlord is appropriately named Mister Beers.

Cross the road and the parking lot to the ***Bull and Chain (2)*** in Langworth Gate, geared for the food trade. Numerous blackboards outside announce special offers, dishes of the day, and the like. Beers are from Tetley's, Bass, and Barnsley breweries.

The stroll past the east front of the Minster through Minster Yard and Pottergate is interesting. Blue plaques on walls reveal the sites of the previous residences of such luminaries as William Byrd (composer and organist of the cathedral) and George Boole (mathematician and former Professor in the University of Cork).

"By this to Lincoln come, upon whose lofty scite Whilst wistly Witham looks with wonderful delight, Enamour'd of the state and beauty of the place..."

Michael Drayton

The next stop is the ❚**Adam and Eve Tavern (3)**❚, a "period" house at the junction of Lindum Hill. Courage Directors and Theakston XB and Best Bitter are sold. A notice on the front door may halt you in your tracks: "Due to excessive wind this door is locked. Please use the rear door through the patio." Behind the parking lot are some play areas. This pub is the headquarters of the Lincoln Petanque Club, and the game is played here in the summer. There is a wide vegetarian selection on the food menu. The building is clearly old, and a board by the fireplace in the front room lists landlords from 1701 to 1935. The stonework and beams are authentic and the ceilings low. Customers can withdraw into numerous inglenooks and

private rooms, or "snugs." The decor is interesting and includes posters advertising shows at the Theatre Royal in Lincoln and facsimile front pages of the *Daily Worker* and the *Daily Herald*.

Amble back up Pottergate to the drinkers mecca: the ❦**Victoria (4)**❦ in Union Road by the west gate of Lincoln Castle. This is clearly where it's all at, as they say. The regular beers listed are mouth-watering enough to keep the average discerning beer buff happy for a lifetime. They include several of Bateman's offerings, Everard Old Original, and Liefmanns Frambozen. The guest beers gild the lily. In addition there is a vast range of British and Belgian bottled beers and a full list of Gale's fruit wines. The menu boards are tempting and the selections reasonably priced; food is served remarkably quickly. The atmosphere is lively, but not intrusive. A kind of reverence pervades the air. The regulars are worshippers, the visitors pilgrims, and the staff privileged servants. All are great believers in ale, but there is nothing pretentious about the place. Two large rooms, solidly furnished, accommodate the congregation.

Top: *The Adam and Eve Tavern.*

Bottom: *The Victoria.*

Tear yourself away and slip around the corner to the ❦**Strugglers (5)**❦ in Westgate. This is a local, but you will be welcomed and included in the conversation. There is evidence in some of the material decorating the walls that the pub dates back at least to 1838. Draught Bass and Fuller's London Pride are on the pumps. This is a drinkers' pub, and while the landlord is a chef who prepares excellent food, it is available at strictly limited times in deference to his drinkers. For example, Sunday lunch is served from 2 P.M. until 4 P.M., after the lunchtime drinkers have had their fill.

At this point you might try a foray outside the city walls and along Union Road towards the Museum of Lincolnshire Life. Find Rasen Lane and the **Lord Tennyson (6)**, a Ward's house that is highly regarded. The food menu is constructed along literary lines inspired by the eponymous poet laureate.

Carry on into Bailgate to the ▮**Duke William (7)**▮, an inn with character, stone-built in a terrace of higgledy piggledy houses. Two large, comfortable rooms are connected by a passageway in front of the central bar, where Wards and Vaux beers are on offer. At the back is a game room. It has been an inn since 1791, and parts of the building date from the 16th century. Dr Marshall, a former Minster organist, claimed that his best compositions were sketched on beer mats in the Duke William while he sipped his

Top: *The Strugglers Inn.*

Bottom: *Duke William Hotel.*

barley wine. The daytime trade is largely tourist and professional, and in the evenings it becomes a yuppie haven. A limited, rather expensive food menu is available.

The Westgate parking lot is nearby, but the crawl could be extended to include Lincoln's classiest pub, the **Wig and Mitre (8)** on Steep Hill. However, be warned, for both the food and the beer in this Sam Smith house are expensive.

89

28

LIVERPOOL

Liverpool is one of the world's great maritime cities, though trade has declined over recent years. It remains a soccer-mad place with great rivalry between the two teams — Liverpool and Everton. Beatlemania is also a potent force in this brash, vibrant, and exciting city. The Merseyside Maritime Museum, the Walker Art Gallery, and the two cathedrals are all worth visiting.

Smartbus #4 travels past the Roman Catholic cathedral, along Hope Street and Catherine Street, down to the central bus station, through the famous Albert Dock, and then onto Sefton Street. It covers most of this crawl. Smartbus #3 goes in the opposite direction. Some of the stops have electronic times of the next bus (hence Smartbus); they generally leave every 30 minutes.

Start at ❦**The Dispensary (1)**❦ on the corner of Renshaw Street and Oldham Street, which is just a few minutes from Lime Street and Central Railway Station. The Dispensary was completely refurbished in 1998 by Cain's, the local Liverpool brewery, as a street corner local incorporating antique bar fittings. It is Cain's fifth tied pub in an expanding estate and the first to be called the Dispensary, a new Cain's alehouse concept. It sells the full range of Cain's beers plus three guests. In addition to the chemist's bric-a-brac on display, there is a wooden Higson's pin from the brewery sampling room, old brewery advertisements, and a huge pair of bellows. It serves good value food from noon until 7 P.M.

"I love Liverpool so much that if I caught one of their players in bed with my missus, I'd tip-toe downstairs to make him a cup of tea."

Koppite

From here, go up Oldham Street and turn right into Roscoe Street, where you will find the ❦**Roscoe Head (2)**❦. This is a Tetley pub and one of the very few pubs in the country featured in every copy of the CAMRA *Good Beer Guide* since 1974. The Roscoe is a completely unspoiled pub with front and rear private rooms, or "snugs," a tiny front bar, and a small main bar. Tetley Mild and Bitter, Ind Coope Burton Ale, Jennings Bitter, and Morland Speckled Hen are on sale. There is hardly enough room on the walls of the rear snug to display all the awards that this pub has won; some are quite prestigious. It is known that the Roscoe has existed as a pub for more than a century after being converted from a house.

Top: *The
Dispensary.*

Bottom:
Roscoe Head.

William Roscoe was a local benefactor. Lunches are available in this friendly local.

Turn right out of the Roscoe and then left up Leece Street, which continues into Hardman Street. Turn right into Pilgrim Street and left into Rice Street. A few yards on is ☞ **Ye Cracke (3)** ☜, a legendary Liverpool pub and one of its most quirky. It has remained unchanged for several years and still has exterior signs advertising for Bass and Boddington's from an era when both these beers were much sought after. Ye Cracke has sold beers from the Oak brewery since it was a local micro-brewery at Ellesmere Port. It also sells Cain's, Marston's Pedigree, guest beers, real cider, and good value lunches. A small front bar, a snug called the "War Office," and other small rooms combine with the cosmopolitan clientele to add to the cozy atmosphere. There is an interesting stained-glass window set in the wall of the main bar.

Continue up Rice Street and left into Hope Street. At the junction with Hardman Street is the impressive ☞ **Philhar-monic Dining Rooms (4)** ☜, where you'll find Tetley beers on the handpumps. The "Phil" is a world famous pub featured in most books on pub architecture. It was built between 1898 and 1900 for the Robert Cain Brewery. It has an amazing wrought iron gateway, and the marble-walled gents' toilets are legendary. There is a public bar, a backbar, two side rooms named Brahms and Liszt, and upstairs dining rooms decorated in Victorian Gin Palace garishness. The dining areas feature engraved windows, ornate ceilings, mosaic tiled floors, and elaborate mahogany carvings. In Brahms there is a stained-glass window that, together with decorative tile work on the bar, is a local feature of Victorian Liverpool pubs. Lunch is available.

Turn left upon leaving and continue along Hope Street. In front of you is the Catholic cathedral (or Paddy's Wigwam, as it is affectionately called), which is open from 8 A.M. until 6 P.M. and is most impressive inside when the sun shines through

the stained glass in the spire. Building started in 1933 with an initial grandiose scheme, according to which only the crypt was completed. In 1962 a new design by Frederick Gibberd was adopted, and the cathedral was consecrated in 1967. The buttresses are adorned with bronze sculptures by local artist Sean Rice.

Below: *The Philharmonic Dining Rooms is on CAMRA's inventory of pub interiors that must be kept. It is featured in the full-color book* Heritage Pubs of Britain.

Also at the end of Hope Street is the ***Everyman Bistro (4a)***, which is featured in the CAMRA *Good Pub Food Guide* for its imaginative menu and good beer.

After the Everyman, turn right onto Oxford Street and then right onto Mulberry Street, where you will find the ❦**Cambridge (5)**❦. Styled as a "Forshaw's Alehouse," it offers the full range of Burtonwood beers plus a guest beer. Being alongside the university campus, it is a popular haunt of students in term time.

Continue along Mulberry Street and then along Catherine Street, past two old Higson's pubs, the Caledonia and the Blackburne Arms. Just before you reach the junction with Upper Parliament Street, on the left is ◦Egerton Street and ❦**Peter Kavanagh's (6)**❦. This Victorian pub's most striking features are the two semi-circular snugs leading off the bar. The pub is named after a designer in the Heath-Robinson mould who designed the two snugs with locking mechanisms used on ocean liners. Some of Peter's patents are on display along with a multitude of quirky bric-a-brac, such as old radios, bicycles, and model cars hanging from the ceiling. The range of beers includes Cain's and Tetley and a couple of guests.

Go right onto Upper Parliament Street towards the massive Liverpool Anglican Cathedral. Designed by Giles Gilbert Scott in Gothic style, the building was begun in 1904 and was completed in 1978. It was built of local stone from a quarry in Woolton, home to the Quarrymen, who went on to become the Beatles. The main stained-glass window, at more than 1,600 square feet, is one of the largest of the 20th century. Carry on down Parliament Street, past the Cain's Brewery to the left, and take the next left, Grafton Street. At the next junction is the ▮Cain's Brewery Tap (7)▮, built in a corner of the Robert Cain Brewery. The Tap sells the full range of Cain's beers plus three guest beers. Once a run-down and neglected backwater under Higson's ownership, it was acquired with the brewery when Whitbread sold it in 1990. It became Cain's first tied pub. Magnificently restored, the new tap, formerly called Grapes, was reopened under its new name in 1994. It was soon honored by an English Heritage/CAMRA award for the best refurbished pub in Britain. It has a fine molded brick and terracotta facade and superb engraved windows. Its interior is that of a Victorian street corner local, unspoiled by those modern scourges of intrusive machines and noisy jukeboxes. The splendid bar counter with its scrolled supports was rescued from a nearby pub about to be demolished, while the rear bar gantry came from an unlikely source — a doghouse. It now incorporates a portrait of Robert Cain, the founder of the brewery in 1850. Note the dog's head carved in the woodwork below the portrait. An interesting collection of "breweryana" adorns the walls, a reminder of long gone breweries, some, such as Threlfall's, Higson's, and Bents, not forgotten. Lunches are available until 2:45 P.M.

If you walk down Stanhope Street to the dock road (Sefton Street) about one hundred yards, there is a Smartbus stop that will take you back to the city center.

29

LLANDUDNO

The description of Llandudno, "a jewel among Victorian resorts," is absolutely right. Nothing much has changed here since 19th-century entrepreneurs established this town. The wonderful beach and the elegant Promenade are crowned and protected from the west by the sentinel of the Great Orme, the summit of which is best reached by the Edwardian tramway. It was in Llandudno that Lewis Carroll told the fantasy stories of Alice in Wonderland to the young Alice Liddell.

The pub crawl takes in five pubs that are very close together in the west end, and one a good 15-minute stroll across town. Start in Church Walks, near the pier at the western end of the Promenade. The first stop is at the ▮**Parade Hotel (1)**▮. There are two bars and a garden, and the pub is typical of the seaside. Beers on sale are Greene King Abbot, a most unusual beer to find in North Wales; Theakston Best Bitter; and a variety of guests. It is open all day.

Close by is the ▮**Olde Victoria (2)**▮, popularly known as the Old Vic. It is a popular, traditional, Victorian house with a homely atmosphere. Victorian photographs of the town adorn the walls. It sells Banks' Mild and Bitter, Cameron Strongarm, Marston's Pedigree, and occasional guest beers. Good value home-cooked meals are available at lunchtime and in the evening in the bar and the restaurant. Attractions include a garden, quiz nights, and folk music sessions. Children are made welcome.

Carry on along Church Walks, turning left into Upper Mostyn Street. A few yards along on the left is the ▮**Fat Cat (3)**▮, a traditional café and bar with wooden floors. Beers on sale are Boddington's Bitter, Theakston XB, and guests. Lunch and evening meals are available, and there is a pleasant garden.

Close by is the ▮**London Hotel (4)**▮ with its Dick Whittington sign. A large central bar serves several small lounge areas. Burtonwood Dark Mild and Bitter beers are sold. One oddity is an old red telephone box. At the back of the pub is an excellent family room that transforms into a piano bar in the evenings. There is a folk club on Saturday, and food is served at lunchtime and in the evenings. Bed and breakfast accommodation is available.

Cross over the roundabout into Mostyn Street and turn right into Market Street. On the right is the ❚**Cottage Loaf (5)**❚ , sometimes called "the village pub in the heart of the town." It was formerly a bakery; the flagged floors are a reminder of this. Courage Directors is on regular sale, and there is a good changing selection of guest beers. A varying menu of food is sold at lunchtime. There is live music on Tuesday and Sunday. Kids are welcome up to 8 P.M.

And now for the fit and thirsty. It is a good 15-minute walk to the next pub, but well worth it. Return to Mostyn Street and turn right. Carry on to the right fork of Conway Road (A470). Go past the first roundabout, and at the second one the ❚**Links Hotel (6)**❚ is on the right. The name comes from its proximity to two golf courses, and incidentally, the building itself resembles a golf clubhouse. There is plenty of room in this pleasantly busy and welcoming pub. The beers are from John Willy Lees of Middleton Junction, Manchester, and include GB Mild and Bitter. Good value food is served at both lunchtime and in the evenings. Bed and breakfast accommodation is available. Kids are well provided for with a conservatory and an outdoor play area. The Links is open all day.

30

LONDON BRIDGE AND THE BOROUGH

There are scores of pubs in the area, and those in this crawl are considered to be the better ones. Six of them are in CAMRA's 1999 *Good Beer Guide*. Because this is essentially a business area, not residential, you will find that some of the pubs are closed on weekends, but there are still plenty open to make the walk an enjoyable one.

The best starting point is Borough Station on the Northern line, which is an easy five-minute walk to Borough Road and the first chosen pub. Alternatively, you could start from Lambeth North on the Bakerloo line, which is a little further away to the west. Buses 35, 40, 133, and P3 stop close by.

❦**The Ship (1)**❦ is on the north side of Borough Road. This open-all-day pub sells Fuller's Chiswick Bitter, London Pride, ESB, and seasonal beers. It is a long, narrow, one-bar pub with ship-related memorabilia adorning the walls. An enclosed outdoor drinking area, running alongside the pub, is open during the summer.

From the Ship turn left into Borough High Street, take the first right into Trinity Street, then turn left on Swan Street and go to the junction with Great Dover Street. Turn right here and take the first left into Nebraska Street. The next stop is the ❦**Royal Oak (2)**❦ in Tabard Street. This is Harvey's first London-based pub, which opened in August 1997 following a major refurbishment, including a welcome return to a two-bar format. As well as a full range of Harvey beers — Mild, Pale Ale, Best Bitter, Armada, and seasonal beers — the pub serves excellent home-cooked food throughout the day, starting with breakfast at 8 A.M. It is normally closed on weekends.

From the Royal Oak turn left into Tabard Street. At the end of the road turn left into Long Lane. Cross Borough High Street and follow Marshalsea Road. Take the third right into Ayres Street. The next pub, ❦**The Lord Clyde (3)**❦, is about 25 yards ahead on the corner of Clennam Street. The outstanding

Top: *The Lord Clyde.*

Bottom: *George Inn.*

feature of this traditional two-room pub is the splendid external tile work, a relic of its former days as a Truman pub. It sells Courage Best, Webster Yorkshire Bitter, Morland Old Speckled Hen, Young's Bitter, and occasional guest beers. It was the 1997 *Daily Mirror* London Pub of the Year. It is open all day except on Sunday afternoons.

From the Lord Clyde retrace your footsteps and turn left at the end of Marshalsea Street into Borough High Street. Go into a courtyard towards the top end of the road for the ❦George Inn (4)❦. This impressive 17th-century coaching inn is currently owned by the National Trust and leased to Whitbread. Beers on sale include Boddington's Bitter, Flowers Original, Fuller's London Pride, Greene King Abbot, Morland Old Speckled Hen, Wadworth 6X, and guests. It is popular with tourists and the local business community and hosts a regular beer festival in the fourth week of each month. The taproom was once used by coachmen waiting for their passengers, and the former bedrooms have been converted into a restaurant and dining rooms. It is open all day, every day.

From the George cross Borough High Street at its junction with Southwark Street. Cross Southwark Street and Stoney Street, and you'll see ❦Wheatsheaf (5)❦ directly ahead. It sells Courage Best Bitter and guest beers and occasionally real cider. This excellent two-bar pub is in the heart of the Borough market conservation area and has recently been

Above:
Wheatsheaf.

granted a Grade II listing. However, the pub is threatened with demolition in Railtrack's Thameslink 2000 plans. The pub is a rare outlet for mild ale, so visit it while you still can and join the campaign to preserve it.

Three doors down, on the corner of Stoney Street and Park Street, is the ❦**Market Porter (6)**❦. This is a large, multi-room pub opposite the former Bishop's Brewery. It is popular with tourists and the local business community. The beers on sale are Fuller's London Pride, Harvey Sussex Best Bitter, and up to five guests. In a time honored London tradition, the upstairs restaurant is open from Monday to Friday for lunch.

The easiest way to get to the next pub is to cut through Borough Market and turn left towards Southwark Cathedral, which is directly in front of you. There has been a church on the site for at least a thousand years, but it has not always known good times. In 1212 it was badly damaged by fire, and it also went through a period of neglect when owned by King James I. In 1604 four parishioners bought the church from him and began to restore it. It was made a cathedral in 1905 and is now full of splendor. There are several interesting features within the church, including a memorial for William Shakespeare and a 13th-century wooden effigy of a knight. Follow the path around the cathedral and go up the stairs to London Bridge.

On the left in Borough High Street is the ❦**Barrowboy & Banker (7)**❦, yet another pub that closes at the weekends. Beers sold are Fuller's Chiswick Bitter, London Pride, ESB, and seasonal ales. The pub is in former bank premises on the approach to London Bridge, lavishly converted into a Fuller's "Ale and Pie" house. There is a large bar on the ground-floor level, and there is an upstairs balcony area. It's very popular with the local business community. There is a good food menu in which pies play a prominent part.

On leaving the pub cross the road, turn left, and then right into Tooley Street. The entrance to Hays Galleria is about 350 yards on the left past the London Dungeon. At the waterfront end overlooking HMS Belfast is ❦**Horniman at Hays (8)**❦. This large waterfront pub, built on the site of Hays Wharf, is open all day during the week, but only from 11 A.M. until 4 P.M. on weekends. Beers on sale are Adnams Bitter, Fuller's London Pride, Marston's Pedigree, Morland Old Speckled Hen, Tetley Bitter, Charles Wells Bombardier, and guests. The pub is named after John Horniman, a local Victorian tea trader who founded the Horniman Free Museum at Forest Hill in London. Food is served in a separate dining area at weekday lunchtime.

On leaving take the time to view the river. Walk past HMS Belfast and go back through Hays Galleria, turning left into Tooley Street. At its junction with Bermondsey Street is the ❦**Shipwright's Arms (9)**❦, which is open all day, every day. This large, former Courage pub was taken over in early 1997 and extensively refurbished. It offers a range of three or four good quality beers that are reasonably priced for the area. Take note of the tiled mural by the bar and the fantastic views of Tower Bridge.

The nearest railway station from here is London Bridge (BR, Northern line and Jubilee line). Buses 47 and P11 go past the door, with many others leaving from London Bridge Station concourse.

31

LOUTH

Louth is one of Lincolnshire's most handsome market towns. There are many fine buildings, and the dominant one is the elegant parish church of St. James, which rises to 295 feet above the flat fenlands. It can be seen from miles around and has the highest steeple in England, except for Salisbury Cathedral. Tennyson was born nearby at Somersby and was a scholar at Louth Grammar School, which he is said to have hated. There is an interesting connection between this pub crawl and the earlier one in Greenwich: The meridian line passes through Louth and is marked by a plaque.

The town has an abundance of fine pubs, and this tour takes in five of them along a linear route with the parish church at one end and the Riverhead at the other. The pubs date from the 17th to the 20th centuries and provide the most dedicated beer drinkers with a range to suit their palates. The railway has long gone from Louth — the nearest stations are Grimsby, Market Rasen, and Skegness — but from all three of these towns, as well as Horncastle and Maplethorpe, there are good bus services to Louth. The bus station is near the center of town, close to the final two pubs on the crawl.

*Below:
Wheatsheaf
and parish
church.*

The crawl starts at the **🍺Wheatsheaf (1)🍺** on Westgate, a street containing many fine Georgian buildings. The pub dates from 1625 and serves beers such as Boddington's Bitter and Flowers Original alongside Draught Bass, Tipsy Toad Ale, and a range of guest beers. This is a beautifully presented and well appointed pub with both the beer and the food of exceptional quality. A word of warning: Watch your head if going in through the front door!

Moving on from here, turn left when leaving the building and admire the splendor of the church spire directly in front of you; it is a truly magnificent sight. Cut through the churchyard along the cobbled road and spare the time to visit this splendid work of ecclesiastical architecture. Pass through the gate, turn right, and beware of vehicles on the roads, which are unsuitable for today's level of traffic. At the corner of Mercer Row turn left and then left again to enter the Market Place, where you will see the ❦**Mason's Arms (2)**❦ in front of you. This building was a Samuel Smith's house until the mid-1970s, when it fell into a state of disrepair. It was bought by Mike Harrison, who restored it to the level at which you find it today. The beer range varies, but normally includes Marston's Pedigree, Bateman XXXB, and Dark Mild as well as a choice of guest beers, one of which, Timothy Taylor Landlord, seems to be making a permanent place for itself. The pub itself is an old coaching inn from the 18th century and provides the customer with a level of service and comfort one would expect from a country hotel.

Moving on from the Mason's, turn left from the front door into the Market Place and take a stroll past some particularly fine buildings, including the spectacular Market Hall, now being used as a shop. It sports a clock tower, superb glass roof, and flagged floor. On Wednesday, market day, enjoy the character and banter of a genuine street market. Go into Eastgate, and ahead of you is the beautiful façade of the ❦**Ye Olde Whyte Swanne (3)**❦, the oldest pub in Louth, built in 1612. The front bar of this pub is a little gem and should not be missed, especially in winter, when two open fires are guaran-

Below: Ye Olde Whyte Swanne.

teed to keep out the coldest chill. The beers are usually from the Bass range, supplemented by a guest beer. This pub is reputed to be haunted, so those of you of a nervous disposition have been warned!

From here take a walk along Eastgate with the church behind you. Pass the Packhorse on your left and carry on until you reach

the ❦**Woodman (4)**❦ on your right. This one-room, basic town pub is handily placed to break your journey through the town. A well-kept pint from the John Smith's range or one of the guest beers will be your reward. There is an impressive collection of film posters and Gary Larson cartoons. Lunches are served every day except Sunday.

Top:
Woodman.

Bottom:
Woolpack.

The walk between the final two pubs passes through an area of Louth seldom seen by tourists, giving you the chance to see more wonderful old buildings. Leaving the Woodman, turn right and walk along Eastgate for about three hundred yards until you come to the war memorial. The almshouses behind this are well worth a second glance. Turn left at the memorial along Ramsgate and follow this road until you come to the junction with Newbridge Hill, where you will see the Wellington. Follow the road to your right and go up the slight incline, which was once an embankment on the Grimsby, Peterborough, and London Railway line. The new houses on your left are built on the site of old railway premises, so you should take a couple of minutes to walk through this estate and admire the old station buildings. This done, proceed over the crest of the hill and walk along Riverhead Road, passing the superbly restored warehouses on your right.

Go past the swimming pool on your left, and about one hundred yards further on you will see the splendid facade of your last port of call, the ❦**Woolpack (5)**❦. Many folks have put forward differing theories on the history of this pub, but the most recent licensee has discovered that the building has been a pub since it was built in 1770. It was a CAMRA favorite in the 1980s, but it suffered a period of decline in the early 90s. It has since regained its former, well deserved status as one of the best pubs in the area. It offers a range of beers from Bateman Brewery at nearby Wainfleet (Mild, XB, and XXXB) along with Marston's Pedigree and a guest beer. It is easy to see the attraction of this pub, especially on a hot summer's day when full use of the very pleasant beer garden is possible. Good value food is served.

The crawl finishes in an interesting part of Louth. Before returning to the town center, you should take the opportunity to have a look around the Riverhead area with a walk along the towpath of the Louth canal, once the busiest in the country, and the River Lud.

32

MERTON & SOUTH WIMBLEDON

Merton is famous as the home of Lord Nelson. He bought Merton Place and lived here in a curious menage à trois with Lord and Lady Hamilton. He left his estate to his mistress after his death at Trafalgar, but she is reputed to have lost the lot through gambling. Merton Abbey was founded by Gilbert the Norman in 1114 near the River Wandle, and it was here that William Morris, the socialist artist, designer, and poet, worked in the late 19th century. Wimbledon is perhaps best known for the All-England Tennis Club, where one of the world's four great championships is held.

Begin the crawl at South Wimbledon Northern Line Station. It may be easier to travel to Wimbledon Station (BR and District Line) and then catch a bus (57, 93, or 155) to the starting point.

From the station cross the road to ⟊**Grove Tavern (1)**⟊, a spacious, modern pub where there should be one guest ale on sale alongside Draught Burton Ale and Tetley Bitter. There is good home-cooked food here. An Irish atmosphere prevails, and there is live TV coverage of Gaelic football matches and live Irish folk music on Sunday. It stays open until midnight on weekdays and until 1 A.M. on Friday and Saturday, when there may be an entrance charge.

Above: *Grove Tavern.*

Upon leaving, follow Morden Road, stopping at the recently renamed ⟊**Princess of Wales (2)**⟊ where, in the view of some folks, you can drink the best pint of Young's Bitter in the area. It also sells Young's Special and seasonal beers. It started a new lease of life under a new name after a concerted campaign spearheaded by customers, residents, and CAMRA had seen off the threat of disposal of the pub (then called the Prince of Wales — one of three so-named in Merton). To think this pub

Top and
bottom:
*Princess of
Wales.*

nearly became a car showroom and repair yard! Of particular note is the outstanding 19th-century facade. Food is available both at lunchtime and in the evenings. The pub closes between 3 and 5 P.M. Monday to Thursday. It is twinned with the Horse Brass pub in Portland, Oregon.

Head back towards South Wimbledon Station and turn right past the parish church of St. John the Divine into High Path. You'll soon see the ▮**Trafalgar (3)**▮ at the junction of the first road on the left. Ask Tom, the landlord, which beer he recommends — he'll probably have about four on tap that may include Draught Bass, King and Barnes Sussex, Gale HSB, Fuller's London Pride, and maybe a couple of guests. Food is available at weekday lunchtime, and the pub is open all day. A ship's wheel is incorporated into a wooden partition that divides the two bars of this intimate pub.

Next carry on along High Path and turn left into Abbey road, stopping at the ▮**Princess Royal (4)**▮ on the first corner. It sells Courage Best Bitter and Directors and Fuller's London Pride; there is usually a guest beer such as Wadworth 6X or Morland Old Speckled Hen. This gem is an early 19th-century street corner pub with two bars and a large, secluded patio at the back. Food is available at lunchtime. The pub is closed from 3 to 5:30 P.M. Monday to Thursday.

At this point, anyone pressed for time can head up Abbey Road to the Nelson Arms (8) and up Norman Road to the Sultan (7), but those enjoying a more leisurely outing should cross Abbey Road and head back towards High Path. Turn left into Station Road then head to Merantun Way, where a controlled pelican crossing allows access to a path leading over the River Wandle into the Abbey Mills heritage site and beyond to the ▮**William Morris (5)**▮ in Watermill Way. Breakspear

Bitter, Theakston XB, and Wadworth 6X are the regular beers alongside a house beer and two guests, one of them routinely from Young of Wandsworth. This pub opened in 1990 in a restored former silk printing works. There are bars on two floors, and families are welcome. Food is available at lunchtime and in the evening in the bars and the restaurant.

Go back across Merantun Way and turn right on to a footpath along the left bank of the River Wandle. This will lead you back to Merton High Street at the pedestrian entrance to the Savacentre. By this route it is fewer than five minutes from the William Morris to the ❦King's Head (6)❦, the stately Young's pub next to the bus garage. There are various claims about how long this former coaching inn has been in business, the earliest date of which is 1496. It has been with Young's since 1831, and it was rebuilt with a new fascia a century later. It is wood-panelled throughout, and there is a family room and a non-smoking lounge. It sells Young's Bitter, Special, and Winter Warmer. Food is available most of the time.

Top: Riverside.

Bottom: Sultan.

From here follow the north side of Merton High Street westward, then turn right into Norman Road. On the northeast corner of the junction with De Burgh Road is the ❦Sultan (7)❦, the only Hopback Brewery pub in the London postal area. Most of the prize winning Salisbury brewery beers are available: GFB, Best Bitter, Entire Stout, Summer Lightning, and Thunderstorm. Sultan was the name of a racehorse, and this pub was rebuilt in 1950 after the original had been destroyed by wartime bombing. A patio adjoins the main bar and the Ted Higgins bar — named after a CAMRA stalwart — which is usually quiet. There are barbecues in summer and occasional beer festivals.

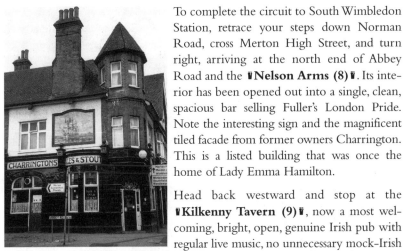

Above:
Nelson Arms.

To complete the circuit to South Wimbledon Station, retrace your steps down Norman Road, cross Merton High Street, and turn right, arriving at the north end of Abbey Road and the ❦**Nelson Arms (8)**❦. Its interior has been opened out into a single, clean, spacious bar selling Fuller's London Pride. Note the interesting sign and the magnificent tiled facade from former owners Charrington. This is a listed building that was once the home of Lady Emma Hamilton.

Head back westward and stop at the ❦**Kilkenny Tavern (9)**❦, now a most welcoming, bright, open, genuine Irish pub with regular live music, no unnecessary mock-Irish paraphernalia, and decent cask conditioned beer — especially Courage Best Bitter. Once you have had your fill, the South Wimbledon tube station is barely 20 yards down the road.

33

NEWBURY

*west of Redding
could take train*

A poem titled "A Nightmare" (probably caused by war whiskey) was supposed to contain the names of all the pubs in the former borough of Newbury. This piece of doggerel listed 75 pubs in its 18 verses and probably dates from World War I. A typical verse went like this:

THE ATLAS TAP didn't care a rap
that THE BELL on the hill should ring.
THE WEAVERS clothed LORD FALKLAND'S ARMS
and I found THE NEWMARKET INN.

Many of the pubs mentioned were actually outside the old borough, and time hath wrought many changes, so that of the five hostelries mentioned above, only one, The Bell, "on the hill" still stands nearly two miles from the town center. But there are still enough pubs left in the town to make a good pub crawl. Indeed, your tour starts with Newbury's newest one, which opened in August 1997.

Arriving at either the bus or railway station, both of which stand to the south of the town center, take a short walk up Cheap Street to the Market Place, where ❦**The Hogshead (1)**❦ stands in the far corner. This was once a local auctioneers' sale room, and the conversion has tried, not always successfully, to retain some of the former character. The entrance is down a long, wide corridor, past a room that used to be the auctioneers' office and which, for some bizarre reason, only has an off-sales license. Consequently, it tends to be used as a meeting room. The long bar that runs along the wall opposite the windows dispenses about a dozen beers: up to eight on hand-pumps and four guests on an eye-level stillage at the back. Regulars include Morland Old Speckled Hen, Fuller's London Pride, Wadworth 6X, and Whitbread Abroad Cooper as well as such continental delights as Hoegaarden Wit and Belle-Vue Kriek on

Below: The Hogshead.

draught. There is a good selection of bottled beers, including Chimay and Duvel, and real draught cider, normally Biddenden. The main body of the pub lies at right angles to the entrance, stretching along the side of the Kennet and Avon Canal, so one can sit on a raised area by the windows and survey the water. The pub is actually larger than the old auction rooms, as the open yard at the far end was incorporated into the building, making a slightly separated section with an attractive balcony also overlooking the canal. The old wooden joists and tie bars in the high roof have been retained, together with various artifacts, but the effect is rather spoiled by the bright metal trunking that runs the length of the interior. The walls are of bare brick and are covered with old posters and documents connected to the former business and the canal. The Hogshead does tasty, good value food.

An even better pub for canalside access is the ❦**Lock, Stock and Barrel (2)**❦. Turn right out of the Hogshead's entrance, past the two continental café bars and the old town hall, and right again over the ancient bridge into the partly pedestrianized Northbrook Street. Immediately on your left is an alleyway leading down to the LSB, as it is known locally. This is a Fuller's pub that opened in 1994, replacing a rather smart, Bass-owned café — a conversion which, strangely enough, caused an outcry among local coffee drinkers! Being Fuller's first pub in West Berkshire, the LSB quickly became the brewery's flagship house, dispensing all Fuller's beers (regulars and seasonals) and good pub food. Except when occupied on a Friday evening with the circuit drinkers, the pub is roomy and welcoming, with a free-standing pulpit for vertical drinkers, free daily papers, and a non-smoking section. The narrow frontage in the alleyway, which also gives access to the canal towpath, belies the size of the L-shaped building. The longer arm of the L fronts a branch of the River Kennet, and customers can sit either on

Below: Lock, Stock and Barrel.

the roof garden or on the patio that runs the length of the pub. You'll enjoy watching the narrow boats negotiate Newbury Lock and the view of the splendid 16th century St. Nicolas Church behind. To the right is a long, half-timbered building that was once part of the Bridge Brewery. The pub's main entrance stands on the site of an old cottage that was the brewery tap. This is definitely a pub for all seasons.

The quickest way to the next port of call is past the old brewery buildings, out of the LSB's back gate, and into Northcroft Lane. Turn left past the Salvation Army hall and take the second turn on the right into West Street. At the top end on the corner is ❚**The Lion (3)**❚. This is another L-shaped pub, which was the town's only free house in the '70s. It was owned by a catering company whose policy was good beer and good food. Following the untimely death of the owner, the pub stood empty for some while, but a spirited campaign by the West Berkshire branch of CAMRA prevented it from being demolished for office buildings. Unfortunately, neglect and the vibrations caused by pile driving for other new office buildings nearby meant that the new owner, Wadworth of Devizes, had to demolish it anyway. But to their eternal credit, they rebuilt the pub in almost the same style, even down to the entrance steps on the corner. The beer range is available according to season, plus a regular guest beer, Badger Tanglefoot, alongside the usual pub food.

The pub's rebuilding has produced more internal space from the same ground area. The long, right-angled bar with ornate decorations in Victorian gin-palace style has recently been turned into an island by opening out the area in the back. As well as plenty of conventional tables, there is an open, wooden-floored area for those who prefer to stand. Perhaps the architectural purists will be pained by the enormous pelmets above the semicircular windows, but the beer drinkers will appreciate the Wadworth beers. The food range includes good toasted sandwiches.

On leaving the Lion, turn right along the other arm of West Street and head back to Northbrook Street. Turn left, and a few yards along on the left is ❦**The Monument (4)**❦. This former Halls of Oxford house was renamed the Tap and Spile after its purchase by that chain in 1995, but many local people resented the change and were very happy when new owners, Century Inns, restored the original name in early 1999. It is the only pub of that name outside of London, marking the fact that the people of Newbury sent aid to the capital after the Great Fire of 1666. It sells a changing range of ales, including the ubiquitous but excellent Tap and Spile Premium. The Monument is a long, narrow building, with the bar on the right and three separate drinking areas to the left separated by partitions with colored glass panels. The renovation of this three hundred-year-old, grade II listed building by the new owners was carefully monitored by the local planners, so most of the interior beamwork is preserved. There are many old photographs of defunct local breweries. The Monument is now the proud possessor of the original sign, which was rescued by a customer from a heap of rubbish behind the pub following the 1995 renovation.

Our final pub is almost back at the start of the tour, but it's worth the walk. Turn right out of the Monument and go along Northbrook Street, then cross over the canal bridge and walk down Bartholmew Street. Just beyond the bridge on the left is Wychwood's Hobgoblin, worth a visit if you have time. The real treat, almost at the far end of Bart Street on the right, is ❦**The Cooper's Arms (5)**❦. This splendid little street corner town local is owned by Arkell's of Swindon, who bought it from Courage in 1992. The locals still have their bar selling Arkell's 3B and Kingsdown together with Noel Ale in the winter. The former owners neglected the pub badly, and it possessed a seedy reputation. To their credit, Arkell's eschewed wholesale renovation: the right-angled bar, which runs around the two outer walls of the pub, and the little private room,

Below: The Cooper's Arms.

or "snug," at the back were kept virtually unchanged. The former game room on the right of the entrance was converted into a pleasant dining room complete with dark panelling and a baronial-style stone fireplace. Much needed new toilets completed the transformation, so the Cooper's is now fit for any company. The dining room in which good pub food is served at lunchtime doubles as a function room in the evenings. No better place could be found to complete your pub crawl around Newbury, since the bus station is less than a minute's walk away and the railway station is just beyond that.

MAP

34

NEWCASTLE UPON TYNE

The city, usually called Newcastle, began life as a fort on Hadrian's wall. It grew into one of the world's great ship-building centers and remains a proud regional capital — live-ly, independent, and as sure of itself today as it was when the "new" castle was built on the site of the Roman fort. In the 1970s it was referred to as a "beer desert." But now, as you shall see, things are very different.

Start in St. Andrews Street, just off Percy Street, beside St. Andrews Church, which is notable for its crooked tower caused by a gun being fired from it during the Jacobite rebel-lions. This part of town once housed Newcastle jail, and this heritage is reflected in the name of the nearby Gallowgate Bus Station and in other buildings, some of which still bear traces of the old prison cells. St. Andrews Street itself was once the site of the prison gardens. Ralph Gardiner, a South Shields brewer, was locked up here for breaking the Newcastle monopoly on brewing beer. He is quoted as saying he was "constrained to drink the gaoler's [jailer's] beer, not fit for human bodies."

"Newcastle is a spacious, extended, infi-nitely populous place; 'tis seat-ed upon the River Tyne, which is here a noble, large and deep river and ships...may come safely up to the very town."

Daniel Defoe

The ❦**Newcastle Arms (1)**❦ on St. Andrews is a Tetley Festival Alehouse that serves a variety of guest beers as well as Tetley Bitter and Ind Coope Burton Ale. It was refurbished in the mid 1990s, when the interior was largely replaced. Food is served at lunchtime.

When you turn left out of the Newcastle Arms, Newcastle's Chinatown, Stowell Street, lies in front of you. Behind Rosie's Bar (formerly the Northumberland Arms and the Darn Crook) is the city wall. Taking this route will take you behind the Chinese restaurants and past Morden Tower, an unlikely venue for poetry reading, but one which has attracted poets from around the globe. Or maybe it's the refreshing pints of ale carried by hand along the alley from Rosie's that keeps them coming. At the end of the alley turn left, keeping the wall on your left, and cross Bath Lane on to Westgate Road.

Above: *Bridge Hotel.*

This follows the course of Hadrian's Wall, although little of this structure is visible in the city itself.

❦**The Bodega (2)**❦ is just beyond the Tyne Theatre and Opera House. It's a former Tyneside and Northumber-land CAMRA Pub of the Year. The pub was previously the Black Bull and was derelict for many years, but it is now in excellent condition, a credit to its owners, the locally based Sir John Fitzgerald pub chain, which owns many of Newcastle's finest pubs. This chain kept cask-conditioned beer flowing in the dark days of the 70s and early 80s. The Bodega serves Theakston Best Bitter, Mordue No. 9 (otherwise known as Geordie Pride), Workie Ticket, Butterknowle Conciliation, and a number of guest beers. Food is available at lunchtime. Note the two original stained-glass ceiling domes. This pub gets very busy when Newcastle United is at home.

Follow Westgate Road past the Assembly Rooms, the monuments to Joseph Cowen and George Stephenson, and the Literary and Philosophical Society. The road will bring you out opposite the High Level Bridge, built by Robert Stephenson, and the castle, built by Henry II. The ❦**Bridge Hotel (3)**❦ is another Fitzgerald pub that has undergone recent renovation. Theakston XB, Boddington's Bitter, and Black Sheep Bitter complement the guest beers. Food is available at lunchtime. From the back of the pub you can obtain a splendid view of the river and its three most picturesque bridges: the High Level Bridge with its two decks for trains and road traffic, the Swing Bridge, and the most recent, the Tyne Bridge, built in 1936.

Walk back to the Castle, go through the Black Gate, and follow the path past the railway arches to Dog Leap Stairs. At the bottom of Dog Leap Stairs is the Side and Newcastle's most famous pub, the ❦**Crown Posada (4)**❦. It was once owned

by a sea captain who installed his Portuguese mistress as landlady. It is notable for its stained-glass windows. This is another quality Fitzgerald pub with no television set, jukebox, or other distractions. Jennings Cumberland Ale, Theakston Best Bitter, Mordue Workie Ticket, Butterknowle Conciliation, Draught Bass, and a guest beer are available to fortify you for the 15-minute walk along the Quayside to the next pub.

The Quayside is undergoing dramatic redevelopment on both sides of the river, with the Baltic Flour Mills earmarked as an art gallery for the new millennium. A Sunday market ('Paddy's Market") still thrives on the Newcastle side of the river, and the offices of the various shipping companies that once operated from the Quayside are still clearly visible. On the left in Lombard Street is a maritime museum. All Saints Cathedral is an architectural oddity that lies a little further from the river.

The Tyne Inn (5), formerly the Ship Tavern, lies under Glasshouse Bridge beside the junction of the Ouseburn and the Tyne, just south of the Byker area of Newcastle in Malin Street. Three Mordue beers, Boddington's Bitter, and Draught Bass are available in this single-room free house that also serves good value, home-cooked food. There is an all-weather garden sheltered by the bridge.

The Free Trade (6) is accessible either by steps leading up from the Tyne Inn or by a footpath. This traditional pub is another Mordue outlet (Geordie Pride, Workie Ticket, Radgie Gadgie), this time combined with Theakston beers (Best Bitter and XB). A magnificent view of the river from the unusual tiered garden is a reward for the climb up from the Quayside.

Head inland from the Free Trade and pass the Ouseburn industrial estate, home to the Hadrian Brewery, now owned by the Four Rivers Brewing Company. **The Fighting Cocks (7)** is the brewery tap. Four Rivers Moondance and Hadrian Gladiator are on sale here, as well as a draught cider. It was the

Tyneside and Northumberland CAMRA Pub of the Year for 1998. This is another pub with a magnificent view. And the jukebox is free!

After leaving the Fighting Cocks follow St. Lawrence Street and skirt around the Byker Wall housing estate. The ❦**Cumberland Arms (8)**❦ lies just beyond a fringe of trees. In an area where pubs are refurbished on a regular basis as a matter of course, it is a delight to enter this unspoiled gem. Local beers such as Mordue and Hadrian are usually on sale, along with popular favorites such as Fuller's London Pride. The pub is also a thriving local music venue.

Below: Ship Inn.

Leave the Cumberland and go down the steps past the city farm to the ❦**Ship Inn (9)**❦. This is another largely unspoiled pub that has Castle Eden Ale and Boddington's Bitter on sale. A climb back up the bank will bring you to either Manors or Byker Metro station. The area is also well served by buses.

MAP

35

NOTTINGHAM

This city that proudly proclaims itself "Queen of the Midlands" is famous for its historic lace-making industry and its Goose Fair. Perhaps it is even more well known for such firms as Boots, Raleigh, and Players. There is much to see here, such as the ancient castle that towers over the city and plays a major part in the legends of Robin Hood. The city was once a major brewing center, and while closures have left it with only one large plant, there are several new microbreweries. There is a wide choice of pubs, as you shall see.

Across the road from Nottingham Midland Railway Station is the ❦ **Queen's Hotel (1)** ❦ in Arkwright Street. Although this is a Greenall's house (a firm not noted for its inspirational pubs), it is well worth a visit as one of the few remaining in the city with a separate lounge and real public bar with a dartboard. It sells Boddington's Bitter, Worthington Bitter, and Draught Bass and has two ever changing guest beers from independent brewers. There is also accommodation.

A short step away in Queensbridge Road is the ❦ **Vat and Fiddle (2)** ❦, selling Everard Tiger, Castle Rock Hemlock and Elsie Mo, Archers Golden, Hook Norton Best Bitter, four guest beers, and traditional cider. It is a simple, one-room pub with separate drinking areas. There is good food at lunchtime and in the early evening. The pub is owned by the Tynemill local pub chain. With tongue firmly in cheek, the name was inspired by the close proximity of the Inland Revenue and Crown Court buildings. The Castle Rock brewery can be seen next door.

Walk along Traffic Street and up Wilford Road. Cross the canal at the picturesque Castle Lock, then turn right at the main road and left into Castle Road. On the left is the Brewhouse Yard Museum and the world famous ❦ **Olde Trip to Jerusalem (3)** ❦. It was built partly in the sandstone caves in the Castle Rock and first opened in 1189. It claims to be England's oldest pub, but there are other challengers. It has recently been gently restored, and although most Nottinghamians approve of what has been done, purists have criticized some aspects of the work. Judge for yourself. Beers

include Hardy and Hanson's Best Mild, Best Bitter, Classic and seasonal beers, and Marston's Pedigree. The pub has a quiet room, an outside drinking area, and a variety of pub games.

Follow the road past Nottingham Castle on the left. On the right is the Nottingham Lace Centre, formerly Severn's Restaurant. This historic building was moved brick by brick from the ancient Broadmarsh area, sadly destroyed to make way for the ugly, concrete Arndale Centre. A visit to the Broadmarsh Caves, accessible from inside the center, is well worthwhile.

Moving up Saint James Road takes you past Standard Hill on the left, where Charles I raised his standard in 1642. Follow the map around to Nottingham Playhouse, where the ▮Limelight Bar (4)▮ will be found on Wellington Circus. Although owned by the theatre, it is run by the same company as the Vat and Fiddle. This bar offers Adnams Bitter, Bateman Mild and XB, Courage Directors, Marston's Pedigree, Theakston XB, and up to six guest beers together with real cider. There is a delightful outside drinking area, excellent food in the restaurant, and occasional live music. Other facilities include a quiet room and a non-smoking area.

Top: *Langry's.*

Bottom: *Bell Inn.*

Next head for Upper Parliament Street and turn left into Sherwood Street after passing the Theatre Royal. There are two adjoined pubs across the road, but you should head for ▮Langry's (5)▮, a Hogshead Alehouse owned by Whitbread. Despite a cheap pine interior, the pub has atmosphere and reliable beer, including Boddington's Bitter, Castle Eden Ale, Chester's Mild, Flowers IPA, Whitbread Trophy, and up to five guests, including a mild and real cider.

Return to the main road and cross into Market Street, which leads into Angel Row and the Old Market Place. Pop into the 15th-century ❦**Bell Inn (6)**❦. A popular meeting point, the Bell has several rooms; the large, windowless room at the rear is a regular live jazz venue. There is also a quiet room and outside area. It sells Draught Bass, Black Sheep Special, Jennings Dark Mild and Bitter, Mansfield Bitter, Ruddle's County, guest beers, and real cider. Meals are available.

Below: Salutation Inn.

Architecture aficionados may wish to break off to walk around the Market Square to view the Council House and the fine Watson Fothergill building on the corner of King Street before returning to Saint James Street. Pass the **Old Malt Cross** (worth calling in if time permits) until you reach Maid Marion Way, once dubbed "the ugliest street in Europe." Walk downhill to the ❦**Salutation Inn (7)**❦. Today this is another Hogshead Alehouse, but the Salutation dates back to 1240. There is a large, noisy front bar, but some quiet, atmospheric small rooms inhabit the rear. Boddington's Bitter, Castle Eden Ale, Whitbread Abroad Cooper, and four guest beers are sold. Meals are served at lunchtime. Upstairs are pool tables and Sky Sports television. Tours around the historic caves and cellars, which date from 900 A.D., are available Monday to Friday at 3 P.M., 5 P.M., and 7 P.M.

On the way back to the station, you may wish to visit the Canal Museum or have a last beer in the **Fellows, Morton and Clayton (8)** in Canal Street as you pass.

Connoisseurs of microbreweries may wish to visit the Bunkers Hill Inn in Hockley, near the Ice Stadium. It is too far off the route to be included in the standard crawl, but it is well worth searching out. It has an ever changing selection of eight beers, almost always from micros, that is reckoned to be the best selection in town. It is open all day except on Sunday and serves good value food.

MAP

36

OTLEY

This splendid little market town is actually part of the metropolitan borough of Leeds, but it is a firmly established, independent place. It nestles in the Wharf valley under the shadow of the Chevin, an impressive hill that gives wonderful views of the lower Dales and the Harrogate area. Thomas Chippendale was born here, and a handsome statue of England's greatest cabinet maker stands in Manor Square in the town center. There is also an interesting monument in the parish churchyard dedicated to laborers who died while building a nearby railway tunnel.

There are 20 pubs in Otley, mainly quite old, and every one of them selling traditional ale. It makes for a good choice for a pub crawl, but if you are not satisfied at the end of it, you can try out most of the rest, for only two are outside the town center. There are good bus services from Leeds, Bradford, and Ilkley, and the bus station is as good a place as any to start.

Turn right into Crossgate, and at the top turn left into Bondgate for the ♦**Rose and Crown (1)**♦. This one-bar pub dates back to 1731, when it was called the King's Arms. The name changed on the coronation of Queen Victoria. It sells Boddington's Bitter, Tetley Bitter, Castle Eden Ale, and a guest beer. Food is available at both lunchtime and in the evenings in the bar and the adjoining restaurant. There are barbecues in summertime.

Turn left out of here, and you will very soon reach the ♦**Junction (2)**♦, a popular free house that is a regular entry in the *Good Beer Guide* (CAMRA, 1999). There is one large bar with tiled floors and some exposed stonework. On sale are a group of regular local beers: Black Sheep Best Bitter, Tetley Bitter, Taylor Best Bitter and Landlord, Theakston Old Peculier, and guest beers. Lunches are served. It has a lively atmosphere and attracts a youngish crowd, although oldies are most welcome.

From the Junction turn left and left again into Charles Street. Turn right into Walkergate for the ♦**Manor House (3)**♦. This terraced pub lies comfortably between shops. It is traditional in every way, unspoiled and welcoming, selling Thwaites beers. Food is on sale at weekday lunchtime.

Turn right out of the pub, cross the road, and opposite, where Walkergate joins Boroughgate, is the ❦**White Swan (4)**❦. It dates back to the 18th century, but apart from the entrance arch, most of the pub was rebuilt in the early years of this century. However, the original stables and the ostler's house remain. The regulars of this thriving pub are a lively lot. The White Swan sells Draught Bass, Stones Best Bitter, Black Sheep Best Bitter, and a guest beer. There is a sun trap of a yard at the back.

Take a right turn along Boroughgate, passing the bus station on your left. There is no reflection of Otley's most famous son, Thomas Chippendale, among the names of its pubs. There was once a Carpenter's Arms, though, where the bus station now stands. It stood opposite the house where he was born. It was later named the Wharfedale but was demolished in 1934. Carry

Top: Bay Horse.

Bottom: Black Bull.

on to the ❦**Bay Horse (5)**❦, a gem of a 19th-century pub that is completely unspoiled. It retains its tiny taproom with serving hatch, alcoves in the lounge, a gracefully curving bar, some splendid stained glass, and a collection of photographs of old Otley. It has a magnificent garden at the back to complement the outside toilets. Beers are Tetley Bitter and two guest beers, one of which will be from a local independent brewery. Basic snacks including "possibly the best beef sandwich in the world" are available for most of the day.

From here go straight across the Market Place to the ❦**Black Bull (6)**❦. This is a magnificent, little-altered tavern that retains an atmosphere reminiscent of medieval times. Today it sells Tetley Bitter, Theakston Best Bitter, and a varying range of guest beers. It may be the oldest pub in Otley, but there are other claimants. It is long and low, white-rendered, and has a proud sign, which, like many others in the immediate area, reflects the rural and agrarian location of the town. The main door to the Black Bull is medieval, solid, and impressive, while inside is a stone fireplace probably dating from its origins. There is also a beautifully preserved bread oven with its original arched brickwork still intact. In its yard are stables, a water pump, and a stone staircase. Much of the present Black Bull is 18th-century, but there is ample evidence that some parts date from even earlier, when it was two buildings. In 1648 a party of Cromwell's Ironsides is said to have called here for refreshment and drunk the tavern dry. Such tales are often apocryphal, but somehow this one seems quite plausible. Good value meals are available during lunchtime.

Go left through the Market Palace. Formerly next door was the New Inn, a splendid Victorian pub with excellent stained-glass bay windows advertising its one-time owner, William Whitaker of Bradford. It closed in 1990 and is now insensitively redecorated in the garish colors of a discount drug store. The windows, sadly, have gone, and the only memory is an area behind named New Inn Yard. Turn left by the cross into Kirkgate, and across is the ♦**Red Lion (7)**♦, a small, well kept pub with three drinking areas served by one bar. Beers usually sold are Courage Directors and John Smith Bitter and Magnet. Food is served at lunchtime and in the evenings; vegetarians are well attended to. There are occasional "happy hours" for seniors.

Next door is the ♦**Whitaker's Arms (8)**♦, the name reflecting its one-time ownership by a long gone brewery from Bradford. Unlike its former stablemate, the New Inn, the Whitaker's remains with its stone flagged floors. Once known as the Dramshop, it has an open plan, albeit in a traditional style. It sells Tetley Bitter and guest ales. There is a garden at the back and a separate restaurant in which food is available at lunchtime and in the evenings. The parish church, with its fine memorial, is one hundred yards ahead.

MAP

37

OXFORD

The starting point for this crawl is Oxford Bus Station in Gloucester Green. The Tourist Information Office is also situated here. Leave by the main road and turn left into George Street. After 150 yards, turn right into New Inn Hall Street, then take the first left into St. Michael Street. One hundred yards ahead on the right is ❦**Three Goats' Heads (1)**❦, the only Samuel Smith establishment in Oxford. It has recently been refurbished, and there are two bars on different levels with lots of polished wood and tiles. It serves good food and, of course, Old Brewery Bitter on draught.

On leaving, continue along St. Michaels Street until you reach Cornmarket. As you look across Cornmarket to your left you will see the church of St. Michael at the Northgate. The tower of this church is of Saxon origin, dating back over eight hundred years, and can be climbed (for a small fee) for an alternative view of the city. Turn left into Cornmarket Street and continue straight ahead into Magdalen Street (pronounced "Maudlin" by the locals!). At the end of Magdalen Street, if you look left into Beaumont Street, you will see on your right the Ashmolean Museum, which houses the university's collection of antiquities (entry is free). Looking across Magdalen Street, you will see the Martyrs Memorial erected in the 1840s in memory of Bishops Latimer, Ridley, and Cranmer, who were burned at the stake in 1555 for following the protestant faith during the reign of Mary Tudor, a Roman Catholic. Cross the road to this monument and turn right after walking past it. After 25 yards, turn left into Broad Street. About 20 yards along Broad Street there is a cross inlaid in the road, which marks the spot where the three martyrs were actually burned at the stake.

On the opposite side of the road is the Oxford Story, where you can ride a mechanized desk through time to learn more about Oxford's history. Continue along Broad Street, passing some of the colleges that make up the university. On your left is Balliol, founded in 1263 and initially reserved for poor scholars (Harold Macmillan, Edward Heath, and Dennis Healey were students here). Next comes Trinity College,

"The clever men at Oxford

Know all that there is to be knowed.

But they none of them know one half as much

As intelligent Mr Toad."

Kenneth Grahame

founded in 1555 on the site of a previous religious institution closed down by Henry VIII.

You then come to Blackwell's, Oxfords famous bookshop. Sandwiched between the entrances to the shop you will find the ❦**The White Horse (2)**❦, a quite small 16th-century pub. Due to its popularity and size, it can get a little crowded. Beers available include Ind Coope Burton Ale, Tetley Bitter, Benskins Best Bitter, Wadworth 6X, and a guest. Lunch and evening meals are available.

On leaving the White Horse, opposite is the Museum of the History of Science, which was the original Ashmolean Museum. It houses a collection of early scientific instruments (including Einstein's blackboard!). Next to the museum is the Sheldonian Theatre, recognizable by the many stone heads on the wall around it. This was built by Christopher Wren in 1664-68. As well as musical recitals, it is still used for its intended purpose — university occasions such as degree ceremonies.

Continue along Broad Street and cross the road to enter ❦**The King's Arms (3)**❦. It is a large, popular, lively pub that has many separate drinking areas — the Don's bar at the rear is worth visiting. A full range of good food is also on offer, and there is a tearoom (for the non appreciators of alcohol) that opens at 10:30 A.M. on Sunday. For those in need of alcoholic refreshment, the choice is good, including a range of Young's beers, Wadworth 6X, and a good selection of bottled beers. There is no live or recorded music.

From here turn left into Holywell Street and walk about 50 yards until you reach Bath Place, a very narrow alley that leads off to the right (if you reach New College you've missed it). Walk down Bath Place towards the Bath Place Hotel, but immediately before its gates, turn left into an even narrower passage (trust me, there is a pub down here!). At the end of the passage you will find the ☙Turf Tavern (4)❧. It is tucked out of the way, but it's certainly worth a visit. This 13th-century, rambling sort of pub has low-beamed ceilings and three garden and courtyard areas that are pleasant to sit in, even during cold weather, due to the practice of having braziers to provide warmth. It has literary connections: It holds a place in Hardy's *Jude the Obscure*. This is definitely one not to miss for the vast selection of beers supplied by small, independent breweries. There is an ever changing range, including Adnams Broadside, Archers Golden, Flowers Original, Morland Old Speckled Hen, Whitbread Abroad Cooper, and up to five guest beers. You can never be sure what might be available. Mulled wine is also sold in winter. The pub serves good food, both snacks and full meals.

Leave by the second passageway, and you will emerge into New College Lane, almost directly beneath the Bridge of Sighs. This is a 19th-century copy of the Venetian original that links the two parts of Hertford College. Turn right and walk towards the metal railings on the far side of Catte Street. From these railings, will see the side of the Sheldonian Theatre directly ahead of you. The building on the left is the Bodleian Library. It has a collection of more than five and a half million books and is one of only six libraries in the world entitled to a copy of each new book published in the UK.

From the railings, turn left and walk down Catte Street, pass the front of the Bodleian, and enter Radcliffe Square, where the Radcliffe Camera dominates the area. This was built between 1337–49 as a reading room for the Bodleian Library and is still used for this purpose. "Camera" is a medieval term for a room. Walk past it towards St. Mary's Church. It was here that the martyrs Cranmer, Ridley, and Latimer were tried for heresy prior to being executed in Broad Street. The church has a high tower that is accessible (for a fee) and provides another good vantage point to view the city. The church also contains a good coffee shop where drinks and light meals are sold.

Once past the church, turn right into High Street and walk past Brasenose College, founded in 1509. It is allegedly named after the original college door knocker, which had a "brazen nose" and now hangs in the dining hall of the college. Just before the junction with Turl Street, you will pass Lincoln College Library and All Saints Church, which was the city church from 1896 until 1975. At this point, cross High Street and walk down Alfred Street and find ▼**The Bear (5)**▼ at its end. It is a very small 17th-century pub built on the site of the original

13th-century Bear Inn. It is famous for its collection of six thousand bits of ties, which adorns most walls and some ceilings. There is a shared courtyard area at the rear of the pub. There is a limited choice of beers — Tetley Bitter, Ind Coope Burton Ale, and Morland Old Speckled

Top: *The Bear.*

Bottom: *The Crown.*

Hen. A visit is a must for the experience, a pint, and a bowl of chips!

On leaving the Bear, turn right into Blue Boar Street and take the first passage on your right. Halfway along this passage you will find the *Wheatsheaf (6)*. Call in if you feel you need an extra stop!

Continue up the passage to rejoin High Street. Turn left and walk to the end, and in front of you is Carfax Tower, the remains of the 14th-century church of St. Martin and a third opportunity to gain a higher perspective of the city! Turn right into Cornmarket Street, walk for about 25 yards, then turn left into the passageway immediately before McDonalds, where you will find ▼**The Crown (7)**▼, the only Bass pub in Oxford. The original inn on this site was several hundred years old, and the present modernized building still retains some old character. There is a courtyard area for the outdoor drinkers. Good food is served.

From the Crown, walk back into Cornmarket street and turn right. Walk to the junction, turn right into Queen Street, and walk its full length, past the shops and the memorial in Bonn Square. At the end of Queen Street continue straight ahead into New Road. On your left you will pass what was Oxford Prison, a typical Victorian building, and the Castle Mound. At the end of New Road turn left into Tidmarsh Lane and follow it into St. Thomas Street. Walk for 25 yards and you will come to ❦ **The Brewery Gate (8)** ❦, immediately adjacent to what until recently was Morrells Brewery. As you would expect, the full range of Morrells products are on offer, although these days they are brewed by the Thomas Hardy brewery in Dorchester.

From the Brewery Gate retrace your steps back along St. Thomas Street and Tidmarsh Lane. Cross New Road and walk along Worcester Street, turning right into George Street, where you will find Gloucester Green Bus Station on the left.

MAP

38

PRESTON

Preston was one of the important centers of the cotton industry — a cradle of the industrial revolution, as it were. The Harris Museum and Art Gallery contains exhibits that tell the history of the cotton trade. Preston is the administrative capital of Lancashire. Every 20 years the famous Preston Guild is held, an event dating from the 12th century, when the town received its charter.

The best place to start this crawl is Preston Bus Station (catch any bus going along Fylde Road). Ask for the ▌**Hogshead (1)**▌, which is your first stop. It opened as recently as June 1995 and was converted from a former doctor's home and surgery that had been derelict for several years. It was known as "Moss Cottage," and this name has been retained on outside signs. It is a large, imposing building set back from the road. Inside there is one large room decorated in the typical Hogshead style, although it does feature a glass wall for customers to view the barrels in the cellar. Regular beers are Boddington's Bitter and Whitbread Abroad Cooper, but, more importantly, there are up to 12 interesting guest beers. The pub was voted CAMRA's West Lancashire branch's first ever Pub of the Season in Autumn 1996; in 1998 it was awarded the George Lee Memorial Trophy, which recognizes outstanding achievement in promoting traditional beers. It's a very popular pub, especially with students, as it is close to the university campus. Food is served all day up to 7 P.M. Nearby in Pedder Street is St. Walburges Church, Preston's most prominent feature and the third highest church spire in Britain.

Below: Lamb and Packet.

Head back towards the town center and cross the large, double roundabout to the ▌**Lamb and Packet (2)**▌ in Friargate.

This prominent white building at the edge of the town center is a comfortable, one-room pub smaller than its external appearance suggests. The regular beers are Thwaites Bitter and either Chairman's Premium Ale or one of Thwaites monthly and seasonal beers. It is a pub that has long been famed for its food and attracts a good lunchtime trade from office workers and students.

Above: *New Britannia Inn.*

The name is derived from a connection between the lamb on the town's coat of arms and the packet boats that used the Lancaster Canal.

Carry on along Friargate and turn right into Heatley Street. On the left is the ❦**New Britannia Inn(3)**❦, a smallish pub with one drinking room and a separate games area. Note the Britannia windows. It is a young persons' pub, very popular with students and bikers, and it gets very busy on weekends. The same family has been in charge for many years, and the pub has been a regular entry in the *Good Beer Guide* (CAMRA, 1999). This is a Whitbread pub selling Boddington's Bitter, Flowers Original, Castle Eden Ale, Goose Eye Bronte Bitter, Marston's Pedigree, and two or three guest beers. Real cider is also served. Some 20 years ago this was the first Whitbread pub in Preston to reintroduce real ale. It has remained popular with local CAMRA members ever since and was the winner of the George Lee Memorial Trophy for 1999. There was once an Old Britannia, which has long since been demolished, on nearby Friargate.

Return to Friargate and turn right. The ❦**Olde Dog and Partridge (4)**❦ appears shortly on the right. This is another one-room pub, but it includes a small separated area for dining and meetings. This pub, too, can become very busy. For some time it was well known as a bikers' pub, and most impressive machines were often parked on the pavement outside. Until 1993 this pub sold only keg beers, but is now another ale-dispensing pub popular with CAMRA members. Regular beers are Worthington Best Bitter, Highgate Dark Mild (mild is rare in the town center), and two guest beers. The pub is known for its good value lunchtime food. The tag "Olde" was recently restored to the pub's name after many years' absence. The pub was the winner of the local CAMRA branch's Autumn 1997 Pub of the Season award, chosen on the theme "the best pub in which to introduce students to real ale."

A little further down Friargate is ❦**Old Black Bull (5)**❦. This very busy but homely pub is prominently sited at the junction

of Friargate and Ringway, which is the main road through the center of Preston. It is a distinctive building with a mock Tudor frontage and tiling around the entrance. A year or so ago it was extended to take over the shop premises next door. Once a Boddington's Bitter stronghold, it has taken full advantage of the guest beer ruling in the 1990s and now sells up to eight guest beers and a draught cider as well. There is a lounge, a private room, or "snug," and a public bar. It is a long standing *Good Beer Guide* entry, and it won the George Lee Memorial Trophy (see Hogshead above) two years running in the early 1990s. It is the only pub in the last 20 years to achieve this feat.

Top: *Old Black Bull.*

Bottom: *Black Horse Hotel.*

Across from the Old Black Bull is the ❦**Greyfriar (6)**❦. This Wetherspoon's pub is very large, even by Wetherspoon standards. It has been converted from a building that was once a carpet showroom, among other things. It is a very busy pub, especially on weekends. It is one of the few town center pubs that currently serves a mild — Thwaites Best Mild is on the handpumps along with Courage Directors, Morland Old Speckled Hen, Theakston Best Bitter, and guest beers. It has all the familiar features of Wetherspoon's pubs, including cheap beers, regular beer festivals, non-smoking areas, and no music.

Cross the Ringway and remain on Friargate until you reach the final stop at the ❦**Black Horse Hotel (7)**❦. From an architectural point of view, this is generally accepted as Preston's most highly rated pub. It is a well preserved street corner house among the shops in a pedestrian precinct. Its features include a tiled bar, mosaic floors, wood panelling, and mirrors. It received an English Heritage/CAMRA award in 1998 for the Best Refurbishment. It is old-fashioned for a town center pub, and there are a couple of rooms separated from the main bar. A good range of Robinson's beers is sold: Best Bitter, Bitter, Frederics, Old Tom, and Hartley XB. The pub has had a regular entry in the *Good Beer Guide* over the past 25 years. It is popular with students and tends to attract a Bohemian clientele. There is no real ale in the upstairs room. The bus station is no more than five minutes from here. Have another?

MAP

39

ST. ALBANS

Where better to pub crawl than in St. Albans, home of the Campaign for Real Ale? With its medieval abbey and cathedral dominating Verulamium Park — site of Roman Britain's third largest town — the city rewards the walker with a rich brew of architecture and beers. St. Albans was one of the first places in England where coaching inns sprang up to provide a resting place for weary pilgrims. At the start of the 19th century, they could shelter some three hundred travellers and stable seven hundred horses. Several of them still stand today, including a contender for "the oldest pub in Britain." When Austin penned his rhyming list, there were more than 80 pubs and five breweries in St. Albans.

If you arrive by train, take the bus from St. Albans City Station to the city center and get off at the top of Victoria Street, opposite the Philanthropist and Firkin, as it happens. Walk up to the traffic lights, cross over, go around the front of the handsome Old Town Hall (tourist information on ground floor), and continue left into Market Place. Fork right down an ancient alley called French Row, where King John of France was said to enjoy a happy imprisonment after failing to raise three million crowns ransom. Pause by the clock tower, built in the first half of the first century, then turn right towards our first watering hole.

"I'll mention the name of each pub in town,

North Western, the Marlborough, the Anchor, the Crown,

The Maltster, the Postboy, the Trumpet and then,

The White Hart, Two Brewers, and the Famous Peahen."

William Austin

❦ **The Tudor Tavern (1)** ❦ at the corner of Verulamium Road and George Street is one of the oldest buildings in St. Albans. This white-washed inn, with an upper storey jutting out over the pavement and typical medieval black beams, was originally a guest house for the abbey. Part of it dates back to 1400, and the impressive crown-post roof still survives. There is also one original window. Earlier this century it was an antiques emporium, but in 1963 it became the Tudor Tavern and had a spell as a sort of steak, sherry, and keg beer house. Today it features four or five real ales on handpumps, including Boddington's Bitter, Marston's Pedigree, Flowers Original, plus, on rotation, Greene King Abbot Ale, IPA, or Wadworth 6X. There is quite a large dining area where you can still get a steak or choose from a predictable menu. It

133

Above: *Ye Olde Fighting Cocks.*

occupies a huge corner site, and there is a wide paved area where tables are set out. The pub is open all day.

Now for a bit of culture. Turn right out of the Tudor Tavern and go down George Street, passing some fascinating antique and craft shops. When you come to the first crossroads, with public bathrooms on the corner, cross to the other side of George Street and turn left down Abbey Mill Lane. Pass the soaring cathedral on your left (well worth a visit) and head through the historic abbey gateway. The road passes the Bishop's Palace and finishes at ▮ **Ye Olde Fighting Cocks (2)** ▮. This unusual, octagonal-shaped hostelry with its high, free-standing chimney, once a medieval pigeon house, is listed in the *Guinness Book of Records* as the oldest inhabited licensed house in England. It had its 1,200-year anniversary in 1993. At least nine real ales are served at any one time, with Tetley Bitter and Marston's Pedigree always available, plus a changing range of guests such as Oakhill Black Magic Stout and Exmoor Gold. Once known as the Old Roundhouse, it actually had a cockpit installed in the 17th century. This area is now preserved as a sunken bar. The cruel sport continued on the premises until 1849, when it was outlawed by the government. There is a plaque on the wall outside dispensing nuggets of history, including the unsubstantiated tale that Oliver Cromwell once spent a night there. What is true is that the pub has secret passages that once linked it to the abbey to help fleeing monks in more troubled times. Hot food is available at lunchtime and in the evening.

The River Ver runs past the pub, and we're going to follow it for a while. Cross the bridge and turn right into Verulamium Park, then carry on with the river on your right and the lake on your left. If you glance across the lake you will see the remains of the Roman walls and possibly two pairs of herons that have taken to nesting on the small island. If you have any bread, the swans and geese will be delighted. At the end of the lake ignore the humpback bridge to your left and carry on

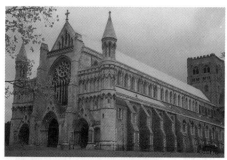

straight out of the park into a little community known as St. Michael's Village. Cross the road and turn left to the ❦**Rose and Crown (3)**❦, another ancient hostelry. This timber-framed building dates back to the 16th century and has been called the Rose and Crown since 1639. The two-bar interior has huge open fireplaces, beams, and cask ales including Adnams, Tetley Bitter, Wadworth 6X, and guest beers. There is a pleasant trellised garden to the side and rear and a fair range of food. This friendly pub, sited at the entrance to the Roman City of Verulamium, does much to help local charities.

Turn left out of the door and, repassing the park entrance, continue over the Ver bridge, pausing to look at beautifully restored Kingsbury Watermill with its massive wheel, built in the 16th century. On the sharp bend, cross into Fishpool Street (a pub on each corner) and enjoy a stroll along the most picturesque residential street in St. Albans. It hosts a hodge podge of architectural styles, and the pavement rises crazily above the level of the road, a throwback to its stagecoach route past.

Top: *The cathedral.*

Bottom: *Lower Red Lion.*

Carry on until you come to the ❦**Lower Red Lion (4)**❦ on your left. This is St. Albans' only genuine free house in which a historic interior is married to a thoroughly up-to-the-minute approach to sourcing ale. The enthusiasts who run it can be relied upon to bring in the newest beers from the newest microbreweries, as well as a wonderful and ever changing selection of cask ales from regional brewers around the country. The house beer, Roaring Success, comes from the small Tring Brewery in Hertfordshire's Chiltern Hills.

Regulars include Adnams and Fuller's London Pride. The old coaching arch leads through to a parking lot and garden at this two-bar inn that dates back to the 17th century. The Lower Red is a favorite watering hole of CAMRA members and was a local branch Pub of the Year. It hosts two annual beer festivals in a marquee in the garden. Good value snacks and light meals are sold at lunchtime, and bed and breakfast accommodation is available.

Above: *The Farrier's Arms.*

Turn left out of the front door and head up the hill. Turn left into Welclose Street, and at the end turn right into Lower Dagnall Street. Just up the hill on your left you will see a pub whose fame has spread well beyond St. Albans. ❦**The Farrier's Arms (5)**❦, a perfect example of a back-street boozer, is set at the end of a Victorian terrace and bears a blue plaque on the wall outside, proclaiming it the place where the first branch meeting of CAMRA was held on 20th November, 1972. The Farrier's is a tenancy of the county's main brewery, McMullen, and serves superbly kept pints of AK, Country, Gladstone, and a seasonal or guest beer. An unadorned public bar is home to pub games, including darts and crib, and the headquarters of two football teams. One step up is the carpeted saloon containing interesting memorabilia and a large watercolor by artist Gail Lilley, wife of former St. Albans MP Peter Lilley. She painted it as a parting gift when they moved out of their home on the opposite corner. Lunchtime food includes filled rolls, sausages, chips, and the like.

From here continue straight up the steep hill to the city center, and you will find yourself back at the Old Town Hall. If you've got the energy, you can turn your back on historic hostelries and visit a very welcome newcomer, a brew pub. Simply walk around the town hall and continue downhill along the main street to a major crossroads with another McMullen's house, the *Peahen (5a)*, on the corner. Turn left into London Road, and a three-minute walk will bring you to the ❦**Farmer's Boy (6)**❦. This modest, one-bar pub suffered a spell as a wine and ale café but was rescued by spirited brewer Viv Davies, who had formerly operated a brew pub 10 miles away in Harpenden. He now has a microbrewery at the back of the premises, where he produces his house beers Verulam Special, Farmer's Joy, and a particularly quaffable IPA. He always dreams up a brew out of the ordinary for St. Albans' annual beer festival run by South Herts CAMRA. The pub also sells Adnams Bitter and occasional guest beers and provides reasonable lunchtime food, including good homemade pies. With a real log fire, the Farmer's Boy is an oasis almost halfway between the city center and the railway station.

Anyone walking back to the station from here can carry on down London Road and turn left into Alma Road, where, for many years, CAMRA had its headquarters in a ramshackle Victorian house halfway along on the right. You will find the city station at the other end of Alma Road by crossing the rail bridge to your right.

MAP

40

SALFORD

If you want Coronation Street and the Rovers Return, then cross the border into Manchester. If you want a crawl of good pubs selling very reasonably priced ale, then stick to the Salford side.

The best way to start this crawl is to take a train from one of the Manchester stations — Oxford Road, Piccadilly, or Victoria — and book through to Salford Crescent. (Salford Central might sound attractive, but it lands you in the middle of the crawl and is only open during commuter hours.) Turn left outside the station and walk along the Crescent (A6) towards Manchester. If your taste is for art, then you are in luck, for on your immediate left is the Museum and Art Gallery in which you will find a fine collection of the works of local artist L. S. Lowry. Spend an hour here if you can, but other pleasures await.

Top: The Crescent.

Bottom: Ye Olde Nelson.

Opposite a bow of the River Irwell, where Manchester racecourse used to be, is ❚**The Crescent (1)**❚, a popular, three-room free house that is open all day during the week and serves food until 8 P.M. University folks like this pub, and the fact that it has been in the *Good Beer Guide* (CAMRA, 1999) for more than a decade is clearly understandable. The beer range varies, but there are never fewer than six cask beers, including a house beer from the Titantic Brewery.

Carry on along the Crescent until its junction with Oldfield Road and spot *The Jollies (2)* just behind the statue of the soldier. It sells John Willy Lees beers. A hundred yards further on and opposite the Roman Catholic cathedral is ❚**Ye Olde Nelson (3)**❚. It is an old-fashioned pub with lots of etched glass,

Above: The King's Arms Ale House.

brass, and mirrors and is described in the *Good Beer Guide* as "a Victorian gem." There are several rooms, and there is an unusual sliding door to the large front vault. This is a good and quite rare outlet for Chester's Mild, a beer that was once brewed just along the road at the former Threlfall's Brewery and known as "Chester's Fighting Mild." It also sells three bitters from Boddington's, Lees, and Whitbread. Overnight accommodation is available and families are welcome.

Continue along Chapel Street, turning right into New Bailey Street. Ten yards along is Gore Street and ♦**The Egerton Arms (4)**♦. This is a free house with a separate vault and a comfortable lounge with a good selection of beers: Holt's Mild and Bitter, Lees Bitter, and Marston's Bitter. The lunchtime food is excellent, and consequently it can get rather full. Coronation Street fans will enjoy the plaque outside the gentlemen's toilet.

On leaving, cross the A6 at the traffic lights and go up Bloom Street. *The Salford Arms* sells Gray's Bitter (brewed by Mansfield) at a very cheap price. But your real destination, ♦**The King's Arms Ale House (5)**♦, is 50 yards further on. This is a listed building, and the interior is completely unspoiled. The bar caters to a large main room; a private room, or "snug," is served by a small counter. Beers from Bridgewater Ales are on regular sale, and there is a house beer, Festival Bitter. Four guest ales along with a traditional cider and a range of Belgian beers are also offered. This classic pub is often used for filming and was seen in the television series *Cracker* and the film *Resurrection Man*.

The next call is not easy to find, but the visit is essential; no pub crawl of Salford would be complete without visiting a Holt's tied house. Turn left from the King's Arms and head up to Inner Ring Road. Turn right and follow the road towards Manchester. When you reach the Renault showrooms, look to your right and there, set back about 50 yards, is the ▮**Eagle Inn (6)**▮. It is known locally as the "Lampoil." This is a classic Holt's back-street alehouse, completely unspoiled with several rooms, a drinking corridor, and typical Holt's prices. There is a Manchester dartboard in the taproom, a small library in the parlor, and more atmosphere than you can shake a stick at.

Below: *Eagle Inn.*

Complete the crawl by walking back to Inner Ring Road. Turn right and, after taking in the aroma of Boddington Brewery, find yourself at the back entrance to Victoria Station, from where you can catch a tram to Piccadilly Station.

41

SEVERN VALLEY RAILWAY

For some good reason, steam railways and real ale seem to go together. So the opportunity to travel on the country's busiest steam line — sampling real ale not only at both terminal stations but also at some of the stops inbetween — makes this pub crawl something different. There are snags, of course. The railway timetable must be kept to, and if the beer at a particular pub is so good that one is not enough and a train is missed, then the next intended stop may have to be missed as well. At best there are 10 trains each day, but on most days there are only six, so you have to be careful. You also need to fit in your journey with the opening times of the pubs.

The best advice is to obtain a timetable by either writing or telephoning the Severn Valley Railway. Reaching the railway is best travelling by British Rail (or whatever it's called these days) to Kidderminster, which has direct lines to Worcester, Hereford, and Birmingham. The two stations are a few yards apart.

The Severn Valley Station at Kidderminster opens early for breakfast in the cafe. There is also a free museum with lots of railway artifacts. In front of the museum is a miniature railway on which children can take a ride. *The King and Castle* is part of the station buildings and is an authentic re-creation of a 1930s station bar and buffet. There is one bar where a wide range of beers is served; regulars are Batham Best Bitter, Marston's Pedigree, Ansell Mild, and a selection from Hobson, Enville, and other local breweries. Meals are served at lunchtime and in the evenings from Thursday to Sunday. The bar closes in the afternoons, except on weekends. There is full wheelchair access, and children are allowed in until 9 P.M.

Below: *The King and Castle on Kidderminster platform.*

Choose your train. Some folks choose merely to travel from one end of the line to the other and sample the beers at the two excellent pubs at the termini. The line runs through the beautiful and unspoiled countryside of the Severn Valley and provides several stops, some close to excellent pubs with others a short, scenic walk away. The picturesque town of Bewdley, which is the first stop, just a quarter of an hour from Kidderminster, has three excellent pubs close to the railway station, forming a minicrawl. Leave by Station Drive and turn right into Stourport Street, then left into Load Street. On the right is ❦**The George Hotel (1)**❦, a town center hotel with a small, popular bar entered from a side passage and a lounge at the front. It sells Ind Coope Burton Ale, Tetley Bitter, and a regularly changing guest beer.

Retrace your steps and turn left into Severnside North. Near the river, with a view of Telford's Bridge, is the ❦**Cock and Magpie (2)**❦, which is a Banks' house in the traditional two-room style. It sells Banks' Mild and Bitter. Summer drinking often spills out into the front of the pub.

Go back towards the station, but at Westbourne Street turn left and go under the railway into Kidderminster Road. On the immediate right is the ❦**Great Western (3)**❦, which sells Banks' Bitter and Mild, Hanson's Mild, Cameron Strongarm, and guests such as Morrells Varsity and Marston's Pedigree. There is a bowl of nuts (real metal ones!) on the bar along with a record of how high people have stacked them. A blackboard outside has some amusing messages. For example, when the River Severn flooded and covered the road, it read: "Warning — big puddle ahead."

Follow your nose for the way back to the station. If you can tear yourself away from Bewdley, then catch the next train north and alight at Arley, which was the star in the recent BBC television comedy series *Oh Doctor Beeching*. Miss the pub, the Harbour, by the river and walk up the hill (about one mile) to Pound Green for the ❦**New Inn**❦. This one-bar pub with several drinking areas serves Banks' Mild, Draught Bass, and guest ales. Live music is spontaneous; piano and accordion players are made most welcome. It is open lunchtime and early evenings, and meals are

served at all sessions. Families are welcome, and outdoor drinking is encouraged in good weather. If you are too tired to climb the hill to the New Inn, then cross the footbridge to the tearooms at the post office. It makes for a change of scene.

Walk back down the hill to catch the next train to the stop at Hampton Loade. Go down to the river and cross it by the wonderful pedestrian ferry. Then walk about half a mile to the ▼Lion Inn▼, a splendid country pub with characterful bars. It sells Hook Norton Old Hooky, Boddington's Bitter, and guest beers, usually from local breweries. The pub closes in the afternoons, but good home-cooked food is served at all sessions. There is a large garden to which families are welcome.

Top: *Pedestrian ferry, Hampton Loade.*

Bottom: *Lion Inn, Hampton Loade.*

Go back across the ferry to catch the next northbound train to Bridgnorth and the ▼Railwayman's Arms▼, which is on the platform. It is in the former station waiting room. In addition to Batham Best Bitter, there are three regularly changing guest beers from small, independent, and often local breweries, a traditional cider, and a good range of malt whiskies. Hot snacks are usually available. The bar is full of an amazing collection of railway memorabilia. If you have time, take the specified crawl around Bridgnorth (beginning page 14). Otherwise, your return train awaits.

42

SHEFFIELD

Sheffield, the steel city, is also the welcoming city. Like many other large cities in Britain, it is taking advantage of the changing tastes for leisure by attracting visitors from all over the world. It is a great sporting and cultural center, and its modern transport system allows ease of movement, particularly between its pubs.

Try this for a crawl with a twist: it's by tram. Most of the way, that is. It starts from Sheffield's main railway station, from where you take a Supertram heading northwest to either Middlewood or Malin Bridge. If you have plenty of time, go all the way to the Bamforth Street stop, and your first pub is close by. If time is limited, then alight at the Shalesmoor stop and start at the third pub. A Day Rider ticket that provides unlimited travel on trams is available and is highly recommended for this crawl.

Above: *New Barrack Tavern.*

Two minutes down the hill from the Bamforth Road tram stop is the ❦**New Barrack Tavern (1)**❦ in Penistone Road. It is a free house that attracts locals and CAMRA members. There are three large rooms and a beer garden. It is usually quiet, but there is live music on some evenings. There are eight real ales including Stones Bitter, Barnsley Bitter and IPA, John Smith Magnet, and guest beers, some of which come from the local Abbeydale Brewery. There is also a traditional cider served. Food is served at lunchtime and in the early evening.

Take the tram to Infirmary Road, and a short walk will bring you to the ❦**Gardener's Arms (2)**❦ opposite the now closed Stones Brewery. This is a genuine free house offering a range of beers from Timothy Taylor of Keighley along with several guests on either handpull or gravity, including a brewery of the month choice. The pub features regular live music sessions and art exhibitions and has one of the few bar billiard tables left in the city.

Above:
*Foundry and
Firkin.*

Get back on the tram for the Shalesmoor stop and the ▮**Cask and Cutler (3)**▮ in Henry Street. It is a free house popular with locals and CAMRA members, including many from outside Sheffield. It was Sheffield CAMRA's Pub of the Year in 1995. There are two rooms, one of which is non-smoking. It serves around six changing real ales from independent breweries and offers traditional ciders. The prices are probably the lowest in Sheffield. There is food at lunchtime and early evenings during the week, but only at Sunday lunchtime on weekends. A beer festival is held in November.

Take a short walk to the ▮**Fat Cat (4)**▮ in Alma Street. This is another free house, frequented by students and anyone else who has the good sense to hunt it out. It is near the Kelham Island Industrial Museum. The Cat was the local CAMRA's Pub of the Year in 1996. There are two rooms downstairs, plus a beer garden, and a function room upstairs. There are 10 real ales on sale, two of which are from the attached Kelham Island Brewery, and a traditional cider. It serves good, reasonably priced food with many veggie options. There is a beer festival in August.

From Shalesmoor take the tram to West Street for the next three pubs. Walk back a few yards to the ▮**Foundry and Firkin (5)**▮, which is part of Allied Domecq's Firkin chain. It is very popular with students and suits at lunchtime and is busy on weekends. This is a bare boards alehouse with assorted game machines and live music some evenings. Beers are brewed on the premises, including some seasonal brews. Food is available up to 7 P.M. There is live music on Sunday.

Opposite the West Street tram stop is the ▮**Hallamshire Hotel (6)**▮, the first of Tetley's Festival Inns and Taverns. Behind the impressive tiled Gilmour's frontage lies an equally impressive refurbishment. Tetley Bitter, Taylor Landlord,

145

and Marston's Pedigree are sold along with two or three guest ales. This popular town center pub can get very busy on weekends.

Cross West Street into Division Street for the ❚**Frog and Parrot (7)**❚, a Whitbread brewpub that attracts town center trade and is popular with students. It has a large, split-level room. The brewery has recently been refurbished, and tours are available. Seven real ales are sold along with a traditional cider. It occasionally produces Roger and Out with a strength of 12.5% abv in both draught and bottle conditioned form. Food is available at lunchtime.

You can either walk or ride to the ❚**Hogshead (8)**❚ in Orchard Square. Leave the tram at the City Hall stop. This is a Whitbread alehouse attracting town trade and is busy in the evenings. It is a small, split-level pub with bare boards and a cafe at the back. Beers include Boddington's Bitter, Marston's Pedigree, Whitbread Abroad Cooper, and three or four changing guest beers along with traditional ciders. Breakfast and lunch are available.

Again you have the choice of a walk or a ride to the next pub, and either way you will go close to Sheffield Cathedral, which has 15th-century origins but was largely rebuilt 60 years ago. In Yorkshire terms, "it's nowt special." By tram alight at Castle Square for the ❚**Banker's Draft (9)**❚, a Wetherspoon's pub in Market Place. It is quite large, as you might expect with the conversion of a bank. There are bars on two floors and non-smoking areas on both levels. Beers are reasonably priced and include Taylor Landlord, Courage Directors, Tetley Bitter, Theakston Best Bitter, and three changing guest ales. Food is served all day until 10 P.M. There is no jukebox or canned music, and there is provision for the disabled. Sadly, after all this good news, the toilets are a long walk away, and there are stairs to negotiate as well.

That's all for this crawl. Take the tram back to the railway station, or walk off those pints!

SHIELDS

43

Nestling on the banks at the mouth of the River Tyne are the twin towns of South and North Shields. A quaint passenger ferry links the two. South Shields is at the heart of the Catherine Cookson tourist area and boasts excellent beaches, an amusement park, the Arbeia Roman fort, camping facilities, the Lea's national conservation area, and the oldest preserved lifeboat. During October the town also plays host to 40,000 competitors finishing the Great North Run. North Shields is the smaller of the twin towns and is a fishing town based around the fish quay. There is a popular water adventure pool and an annual arts festival, and it is the car ferry terminal for Scandinavia and Germany. Both towns are well served by the local Metro train and bus services.

Top:
Chichester Arms.

Bottom:
Dolly Peel.

Out of town visitors may wish to make use of the Day Rover ticket for travel on all buses, the Metro, and the ferry. It costs £3.50 and can be bought from tourist information centers and major Metro stations.

Start in South Shields at the Chichester Metro Station. Turn left into the first stop, the ⏃**Chichester Arms (1)**⏃. This town house has a large bar and comfortable lounge and serves good value, home-cooked meals until 2 P.M. The ales on offer are Tetley Bitter, Ind Coope Burton Ale, and two guest beers.

Head back and through the Metro station, turn right into Beaufront Terrace, and follow the road around and down Laygate. Continue past the roundabout and through the small shopping area. At the junction of Laygate and Commercial Road you will find the *Good Beer Guide* (CAMRA, 1999) listed ⏃**Dolly Peel (2)**⏃ on the left. This two-room pub is named after a legendary fishwife turned smuggler who had many run-ins with the local press gangs. It sells Taylor Landlord, Courage

147

Directors, Black Sheep Special, a house beer from Durham Brewery, and two guest ales. Snacks and sandwiches can also be had. Of interest is the three-lanterned street light in the main bar.

Head down Commercial Road, passing the new courts and police station on the right, and come to ❦**Riverside Public House (3)**❦ at the top of the Mill Dam conservation area. "Beers from around the UK" is the slogan on the shirts of the smartly uniformed staff. Permanently on sale are Taylor Landlord, Courage Directors, Theakston Best Bitter, and three guest ales. Also available are real cider, snacks, and sandwiches. Nearby in Coronation Street and worth a visit if time permits is the *Steamboat (4)*, a nautical pub steeped in tradition. It sells Vaux beers.

Head towards the Market Place, where you will see the old town hall sitting squarely in the middle. Take the first left at the roundabout into Ferry Street, and on the left you will find the ❦**Alum Ale House (5)**❦. This is one of the oldest buildings in South Shields, with records dating back to 1763. Up to 1936 it was the William Wood's Brewery tap, but then it was used as offices in the local lead mining industry. The Alum was reborn in 1993 and features an open-plan bar area with a downstairs function room cum cellar jazz club. Beers on offer are Cameron Strongarm, Banks' Bitter, and Marston's Pedigree along with three guest ales. Food is simple — snacks, sandwiches, and soup.

Turn right out of the Alum, heading to the river and the new ferry landing. Take the passenger ferry to the Royal Quays (for the shops and water amusement park) and to North Shields. Ferries from South Shields leave at quarter past and quarter to the hour throughout the day, except on Sunday evenings. The journey takes about seven minutes, and excellent views of the industrial banks of the Tyne can be seen.

Alighting at the ferry landing, turn right along New Quay and you will find the ❦**Port Hole (6)**❦. This nautically themed pub offers good value food at both the bar and in

Above: *Ferry across the Tyne.*

the small restaurant. It sells Theakston Best Bitter, Courage Directors, and a national guest beer that is usually either Marston's Pedigree or Fuller's London Pride.

Go left along Clive Street then up the steps to the ▼**Magnesia Bank (7)**▼ in Camden Street. This CAMRA award winning pub overlooks the Tyne. It was once a bank and then a club, and the building lay derelict until 1990, when it was refurbished to its present excellent state. It is now renowned for a wide selection of beers served in oversized glasses and also has a reputation for fine food. Local brewers are always well represented in the pub: Durham Magus, Mordue Workie Ticket and Maggie Mayhem, and Castle Eden Nimmos XXXX are staples accompanied by a variety of guest beers. An open-plan interior provides a number of separate areas for eating and drinking in comfort. The pub has a diary of monthly events, including live music in the bar and in the upstairs Bank Suite. There is a montage of photographs of the Lindisfarne folk group as well as old theatrical flyers on the walls of the pub.

The trail heads westward past the *Garrick's Head (8)*, an excellent refurbishment of what used to be a garish disco bar. Beers include Draught Bass, Morland Old Speckled Hen, Courage Directors, John Smith Bitter, and a guest. Another excellent refurbishment just off our trail is the *Colonel Linskill (9)* in Charlotte Street. It sells Taylor Landlord and up to six guest ales. The trail now goes north, across Tynemouth Road, to the ▼**Tap and Spile (10)**▼. This was called the Victoria before opening as the region's second Tap and Spile in the late 1980s. This two-room pub always seeks to provide a range of locally brewed beers and a combination of session beers and higher gravity ales and cider. It is rated as one of the best in the Tap and Spile range. The beer range varies but often includes a choice from Hambleton and Durham. It serves food at lunchtime.

Follow Tynemouth Road towards Tynemouth and continue down the hill to the ❦ **Tynemouth Lodge (11)** ❦, a free house that was built in 1770. The pub is actually in Tynemouth, although the road sign would have you believe you are still in North Shields. Belhaven 80/-, Draught Bass, and occasional guest beers are on the beer menu in this two-room, comfortable hostelry that can get busy on weekend evenings.

The adjoining buildings are under the same ownership as the Tynemouth Lodge and have their own blue plaque explaining that the living quarters of the pub were once a kitchen providing sustenance for the House of Correction next door. Beyond the pub is the Governor's Tree, where another blue plaque outlines the history of this site dating back to the time when the Pow Burn was a navigable river and ran along the course of what is now Tynemouth Road.

To get to Tynemouth Station, go past the architecturally impressive Master Mariners Asylum, built in the mid-19th century as North Shields and Tynemouth began their rise to industrial prominence as port and resort for the Tyneside conurbation. Carry on along Tynemouth Road and bear left for the station. Newcastle is about 20 minutes by Metro through North Shields, or half an hour using the coast route and through Gosforth.

MAP

44

STALYBRIDGE

Stalybridge was one of the most important cotton towns of the Greater Manchester area and also was in the heart of the Chartist movement. Frederick Engels, the political theorist and friend of Karl Marx, often visited the town and described it as a "…disgustingly filthy town…in a beautiful setting."

Unique is a word that cannot be qualified, and this crawl is unique. The "Stalybridge Eight" starts at the pub with the shortest name in the United Kingdom and finishes at the one with the longest. Both these pubs are recognized in the *Guinness Book of Records*. Beat that! And you can record your crawl by buying a passport at the first pub and having it stamped at each pub on the way.

❦**The Q (1)**❦, which is close to Stalybridge Railway Station, started life as a mill manager's residence in 1785. It has had various lives — the contents from its period as a shoemaker's shop are in a local museum. Marston's Bitter and Pedigree are on regular sale here along with at least three guest beers. Sandwiches and bar snacks are available and a traditional Sunday lunch is served. There is jazz on Monday evenings. Be sure to visit the upstairs cocktail bar and conservatory.

Move across the Stalybridge Station platform to the ❦**Station Buffet (2)**❦. Although it is not the only buffet bar of this sort and can make no claim to uniqueness, it is the best known and best loved of the genre. It has remained unchanged since 1885, and there was a forerunner dating from 1845. Records show that in the 1870s a local man was given seven days hard labor for pinching a glass worth sixpence from the bar. Attempts by the rail authorities to demolish the property a few years ago met with fierce opposition from many folks, including the local CAMRA branch. A high quality refurbishment followed, which, ironically, received an award for the best heritage work on a railway building. It has also been extended and now boasts two bars. It has also won the Best Refurbishment category in the English Heritage/CAMRA pub design awards. On regular sale are Boddington's Bitter, Wadworth 6X, and Flowers IPA along with up to six guest beers, a traditional cider, and bottled beers from Belgium. Bar snacks are available,

Above: *White House.*

including the famous black peas. Saturday is folk night, for which big crowds from far and wide assemble. There are periodic beer festivals.

Retrace your steps, passing the Q Inn, to nearby ❦**Rose and Crown (3)**❦, built in 1845. In 1892 it was bought by Shaw's of Dukinfield, a brewery that was taken over by John Smith's of Tadcaster in 1941. Vaux Mild, Bitter, and Samson are sold here with regular guest beers and seasonal specials. This is a friendly pub that has been tastefully restored to respect its history. At one time this and the many other pubs in Market Street — there were more than 40 of them — served the workers in the town's cotton mills. Now it has a loyal band of locals who enjoy its atmosphere; it is a hub of community life.

Turn right and move along Market street to the ❦**Old Fleece (4)**❦. It was built as a coaching inn in 1803 and called the Golden Lion. The present name dates from 1842. In 1860 Sam Hurst, the "Stalybridge Infant," lived here. He was a champion prize fighter with an awesome reputation that lasted until, following a good night out, he fell down the backyard steps and never recovered his championship form. John Smith's and Boddington's bitters are sold in this busy town center pub, and there is a wide range of bar snacks. The pub is open all day during the week.

Walk a few yards along Market Street, turning right into Water Street for the ❦**White House (5)**❦. The fine old building started life as a woollen clothiers in 1729 and a century later became a wine and spirits merchant. Ten years later it became a pub known as Heap's Vaults, named after the owner, and has remained in the same business for more than a century and a half. This enterprising house is friendly and popular and has something for everybody. Choose to drink in either the front parlor, the main lounge, or the bar and game room. Marston's Bitter and Pedigree and Thwaites Bitter are on regular sale with up to five guest beers. There is also a selection of 50 foreign bottled beers, 50 malt whiskies, and snacks and sandwiches served all day. There is a folk club on Thursday evenings. To add to your pleasure, the pub has a friendly ghost!

Water Street leads into Caroline Street, and here on the right is the ❦Wellington Inn (6)❦. This is a popular town center pub dating from 1856, when it opened as an alehouse. Not much has changed; it retains two rooms — a lounge and a taproom — and beer is all important. Boddington's Bitter is on sale, and sandwiches are available at lunchtime. The pub is open all day except Sunday, when it shuts down during the afternoon.

Go to High Street, turn left, and along Kenworthy Street on the right find the ❦Pineapple (7)❦. The pub opened in 1837, the year of Queen Victoria's coronation. The owner was John Kenworthy, who probably built the street and named it after himself, a common practice in those days. This stone-built pub has three comfortable rooms and sells beers from Robinson's — always the Best Bitter and maybe the Hatters Mild. There are sandwiches and bar snacks and a traditional Sunday lunch. The pub is open all day on Friday and Saturday.

Below: The Old Thirteenth Cheshire Astley Volunteer Rifleman Corps Inn.

Turn left on leaving the pub, then take the first right. Take the first left and follow the road around until you reach Astley Street, and on the right is ❦The Old Thirteenth Cheshire Astley Volunteer Rifleman Corps Inn (8)❦. It is a bit of a mouthful and a bit of a walk, but well worth it in the end. It is officially recognized by the *Guinness Book of Records* as the pub with the longest name in Britain, with 55 letters. This

delightful Victorian terraced inn with great views over the town first opened as a beer house in 1855. It is close to the drill hall for the volunteer militia, the forerunner of the Territorial Army. The militia's job was somewhat different from the TA's, for they were required to put down civil uprisings and were often used in Stalybridge during the Chartist riots. There are many photographic memories of the area in former times and much military memorabilia. John Smith Bitter and a couple of guest beers may be on sale, but the beer range is flexible. The pub opens from 3 P.M. (sometimes earlier) until 11 P.M. except Sunday, when it closes during the afternoon. This is a friendly and welcoming pub and a good choice to end the crawl on. Now take a gentle stroll back to the railway station. Perhaps there may be time for another pint.

At the time of writing this book, Stalybridge was going through a pub boom with a number of new pubs opening. Much of this activity is associated with the completion of the restoration of the Huddersfield Narrow Canal and the anticipated tourist trade. Two of the new pubs are on the route of this crawl. Between the Rose and Crown (3) and the Old Fleece (4) is the *Pavilion*, which is described as being decked out in traditional Victorian style. And between the White House (5) and the Wellington (6), a former plumbers' premises have become the *Bridge Inn*, under the same ownership as Q and the White House.

45

STOCKPORT

Although historically a part of Cheshire, Stockport is one of Manchester's major satellites. Essentially it is an industrial town that has suffered extensive redevelopment, but it retains some areas of surprising character and historic interest, especially around the market place. Stockport is the home of Robinson's, one of the largest remaining family brewers. The brewery stands on a cramped site right in the town center. The town also boasts one of the finest selections of unspoiled pubs in the country, with five entries on CAMRA's National Inventory of Pub Interiors within a mile of the town center, three of which are visited on this crawl.

The town is dominated by the gigantic viaduct that dates from 1840 and claims to be the largest brick structure in the world. It carries the main Manchester to London railway line across the steep-sided valley of the River Mersey. Right under the viaduct on Heaton Lane is your first pub, the ☗**Crown (1)**☗, which once enjoyed the splendid description in the *Good Beer Guide* (CAMRA, 1999): "Awesome view of the viaduct from the outside gents." Inevitably, the wind of change has altered this, and the toilets are now inside —whether this constitutes progress is up to you. The former multi-room character of the pub has been eroded by being opened up a little, but it retains a distinct vault and three drinking areas, opening off the main bar, that would qualify as separate rooms were it not for the absence of doors. When owned by Boddington's it was converted to an alehouse format, and since then it has offered the widest choice of real ales in Stockport, with up to 10 available at any one time. Featured are local micros such as Phoenix and Whim. However, choice has not been achieved at the expense of quality, and the Crown appears regularly in the *Good Beer Guide*. It can be quiet at lunchtime but becomes very busy and lively in the evenings, especially towards the end of the week.

From the Crown turn left up Heaton Lane, then cross the A6 in Mersey Square by Debenham's and continue straight down Princes Street to reach the ☗**Swan With Two Necks (2)**☗ on your left. This small pub is in a terrace of shops and is a rare survivor in the kind of location where pubs are increasingly being turned over to retail use. It has an unspoiled 1920s interior making extensive use of light oak panelling. The superb, top-lit private room, or "snug," behind the bar is the best feature. Robinson's Hatters Mild and Best Bitter are available on handpump. In contrast to the Crown, the Swan can be very busy at lunchtime but is often quieter in the evenings. It closes early on Monday and Tuesday.

Follow Princes Street along to the end, where you could put your nose around the door of the *Tiviot (3)*, another Robinson's pub, altered rather more than the Swan, but still retaining an atmosphere reminiscent of pubs thirty or forty years ago. It is popular with older regulars, particularly at lunchtime.

To skip this pub after leaving the Swan, turn right to pass through a small paved square at the end of the Merseyway shopping precinct. Carry straight on along Bridge Street, then follow the road around to the right along Great Underbank. On the right along here is Underbank Hall, a 16th-century half-timbered mansion that now forms part of the Natwest Bank. At the small roundabout by the White Lion, turn left up Little Underbank, and the ♥**Queen's Head (4)**♥ is on your right, just before the bridge that carries St. Petersgate across the street. This is another small, single-fronted pub that is also known as Turner's Vaults, which goes back a long way. Into the late 1980s it retained an interior that had changed in few respects for 150 years. It was then in such poor repair that the new owners, Sam Smith, had to effectively gut it and rebuild it as new. But the end result is so convincing that you would never guess it is not original. It was the deserved winner in 1991 of a CAMRA Award for Pub Conservation. There are three rooms: a convivial front bar with a counter adorned by a wonderful set of spirit taps; a small, cozy, wood-panelled "news room"; and a slightly larger and smarter rear lounge. The only real ale available is Sam Smith Old Brewery Bitter, but you can also sample their extensive range of distinctive bottled beers.

On the opposite side of the street, just past the bridge, Stockport town center has recently gained its first Holt's outlet,

❦ Winters (5) ❦. This former jeweler's shop had a checkered career as a wine bar before passing to Holt's in 1998. They have done an excellent job of refurbishing it, with a down-to-earth vault on the ground floor and a more comfortable lounge upstairs, from where the workings of the superbly restored clock can be viewed. Holt's Mild, Bitter, and the premium beer DBA are available at Holt's bargain prices.

Return to the Queen's Head, then take the steep flight of steps immediately opposite the pub. These lead up to the level of St. Petersgate and the Market Place. Dominated by the impressive iron and glass Victorian Market Hall, Stockport's Market Place is also home to five pubs, four of which are the centers of the live music scene in the town. All have their merits, but the pick of the bunch is undoubtedly the **❦ Baker's Vaults (6) ❦** on the left, an impressive free-standing pub built in the Italianate style in the 1840s. The interior is basically one large room, but it is divided by the central bar counter into distinct vault and lounge sides. On first entering, you could be forgiven for thinking that no real ale is available, as the bar sprouts nothing but continental-style T-bars. But rest assured, the Robinson's Hatters Mild and Best Bitter are definitely real, dispensed through free-flow electric pumps. A wide selection of high quality, homemade food is available at lunchtime, when the pub is very popular with shoppers. Most evenings, when its character changes into that of a buzzing live music venue mainly featuring R'n'B and jazz, it gets extremely busy.

Coming out of the Baker's Vaults, go straight ahead along the left side of the Market Hall until you reach the parish church. Then turn left down Millgate, and the **❦ Arden Arms (7) ❦** is on your left by the miniroundabout. This is a brick corner pub dating back to the 1830s. Robinson's Hatters Mild, Old Stockport, and Best Bitter are dispensed from handpumps set against the back wall of the bar. Arden retains a feature of early Victorian pubs that is exceptionally rare and may now even be unique — namely, a delightful, intimate snug at the rear of the bar that is part of the public drinking space, but can be reached only by walking through the serving area. The bar itself, partially encased by windowed panels, is another fine traditional element. There's also a lobby with an original tiled floor, a lounge on the apex of the building, and another lounge that has been created by extending the former vault. Despite its outstanding architectural features, the Arden Arms is a busy, down-to-earth local.

Turn left outside the Arden Arms, pass under the bridge linking the Asda superstore to its parking lot, and turn right at the traffic lights along Great Portwood Street. Your final call, the **Railway (8)**, is about two hundred yards along on the left, opposite a row of modern superstores. This pub went through various tacky incarnations as "Cheekies" and "Byrons" and seemed destined for closure until it was rescued in 1996 by Dave Porter, owner of the eponymous microbrewery based in Haslingden. It has now reverted to its original name — which relates to the old Cheshire Lines Railway that once ran through this part of the town — and has been transformed back into a proper pub. It has a fairly plain and unassuming single bar, but it is clean, pleasant, comfortable, and welcoming with good homemade food at lunchtime. The chief attraction is the beer, as it sells the full range of Porter's excellent, distinctive beers: Mild, Bitter, Rossendale Ale, Porter, the dangerously drinkable Sunshine, a house beer called Railway Sleeper, various one-off brews, and real cider. The prices are very reasonable. Not surprisingly, the Railway has rapidly established itself as a favorite amongst Stockport drinkers and can have a lively atmosphere in the evenings. It is open all day apart from Sunday and bank holidays, when it closes in the afternoon.

The Railway is a 15- to 20-minute walk from both the bus and rail stations and, for the extremely lazy, is served by numerous buses from Stockport in the direction of Brinnington and Bredbury.

SWINDON

46

Swindon is a town of two centers. Near the railway station is New Swindon, dating from the 1840s onwards and inextricably tied up with the fortunes of the Great Western Railway works. At the top of the hill is Old Swindon, formerly a small market town with its success based on limestone quarries. The coming of the canal in the 1790s boosted the output of stone and brought a spell of prosperity to the town. An unfortunate side effect was that all the old pubs were rebuilt, and there is nothing in this part of town that one could now call quaint or old-fashioned.

After the repeal of the Beerhouse Act in 1869, the magistrates were very strict, and few new pubs opened. In fact, Swindon, with three times its population, had a similar number of pubs to Salisbury. Consequently, brewers have over the years concentrated their money into the comparatively few pubs in the town so, sadly, no original interiors remain. Nevertheless, there are some pubs of character, though their existence is probably more due to accident than design!

From the railway station turn right and walk towards the Railway Village, which was built to accommodate the first employees of the works. Adjoining the sadly derelict Mechanics' Institute in Emlyn Square is the ❦**Glue Pot (1)**❦, Archers only tied house in Swindon. It originated as a grocers and beer shop in the 1850s and was later known as the London Stout Tavern. It is a cheerful one-bar pub with a mainly local clientele. It keeps the full range of Archers beers and a guest beer. Meals are served at lunchtime. Possibly because this is a listed building, the keg dispensers are hidden under the bar!

Above: *Glue Pot.*

Just to the west of the Mechanics' Institute is the ❦**Baker's Arms (2)**❦, another listed building and former beer shop. This was also a bakery, and remains of the oven may be found in the

159

cozy little backbar, along with a fine, large scale model of a GWR locomotive. Once again, this is a locals' pub and serves good pints of Arkell's 2B and 3B, the other local brewer's beer. There is live music on weekends. The nearby **Cricketers (3)** was the only purpose-built pub in the Railway Village and serves Ushers beers. It is very popular with the gay community. It is yet another listed building!

It's now a bit of a trek to the next pubs, which are situated halfway between the Old and New Towns. It's best to follow the map than to be confused by intricate directions! ☙**The Duke of Wellington (4)**☙ in Eastcott Hill is the only Arkell pub that serves beer (2B and 3B) by gravity direct from the cask. It is a small locals' pub with a bar and a tiny private room, or "snug." It has interesting origins. The noble duke was the originator of the Beerhouse Act of 1830. Under this act, any householder could sell beer without recourse to the magistrates. By 1869 the temperance movement was rampant and the act was to be repealed. On learning this, John Arkell bought two newly constructed houses, knocked them into one, and opened them as a beerhouse just in time to avoid the new legislation. As a tribute to a national hero and as a dig at the temperance movement, he named the pub in the Duke's honor!

Top: *Baker's Arms.*

Bottom: *The Duke of Wellington.*

The *George (5)*, next door to the Duke of Wellington, is the oldest surviving pub building in Swindon, dating from the middle of the 18th century, but it was not a pub until after 1830 (prior to that it was a farm). It sells Courage Best Bitter, Marston's Pedigree, and Wadworth 6X.

It is but a short walk (make three right turns) to the ☙**Beehive (6)**☙ in Prospect Hill, one of only two Morrells pubs in Swindon. Possibly the town's most characterful (and character-full) pub, it comprises a series of small rooms. It is situated on a steep hill, with every room on a different level. Beers are Morrell's Varsity Bitter and a guest beer. The pub is the haunt of fans of all ages — 18 to 70 — especially bikers and boozers. Sunday lunchtime features rock bands. Charlie Watts played here once.

Wander down Union Street into Albert Street for the ❦**Rising Sun (7)**❦, which is just behind the newspaper offices. This is a small, stone-built, back street local dating from the 1840s, when it was known as the Heart in Hand. However, to all Swindonians, it's the Roaring Donkey, apparently named after the beast that a landlord kept in the backyard many years ago. It enjoys a mainly local trade and offers the full Usher beer range along with Courage Best Bitter and real draught cider. There's a busy public bar with a pool table and a tiny flagstone-floored lounge. It is open all day.

Just around the corner in Wood Street is the ❦**King's Arms Hotel (8)**❦, a busy, single-bar hotel that sells Arkell's 2B, 3B, and Kingsdown and serves lunch and evening meals. It is a listed building. The original building dates from 1835, when it was also a bakery. Overnight accommodation is available and, bearing this in mind, it is worth mentioning that there are some excellent village pubs near Swindon. Well worth a visit are the Carters Rest and Check Inn in Wroughton and the Plough, Harrow, and Black Horse in Wanborough.

Above: *King's Arms Hotel.*

MAP

47

TAFF VALE

Visitors to Wales tend to head for the mountains or the coast. This pub crawl near Cardiff captures the spirit of South Wales. It takes you through the narrow pass where the hills of the old mining valleys reach down to the edge of the capital city on the coastal plain. On one side the tight entrance of the Taff Valley is guarded by the romantic towers of Castell Coch (the Red Castle); on the other rises up the Garth, celebrated in the film *The Englishman Who Went Up A Hill And Came Down A Mountain*.

It is an area steeped in industrial history, yet it has startling scenery. And of course, it boasts some good pubs. This lengthy crawl takes in six. Those seeking a less strenuous challenge could omit the first two in Tongwynlais. Those wanting only a short stroll can visit only the last three.

To reach the start, take the Valleys Line from Cardiff Central Station. Trains for Treherbert, Merthyr Tydfil, and Aberdare all pass this way. Those wishing to enjoy a pleasant half-hour riverside stroll to the first pub should get off at Radyr Station. Otherwise continue to the next stop at Taffs Well and walk back to Tongwynlais.

If you start at Radyr, cross over the river by the footbridge alongside the station and turn left along the Taff Trail. After passing a wide weir and going under the M4 motorway to reach an iron footbridge (giving good views of Castell Coch), turn away from the river up a tarmac road. At the top turn right and then left under the A470. At the end of the street turn left into the center of Tongwynlais and find the first pub.

By the path to Castell Coch stands the historic ❚**Lewis Arms (1)** ❚. As you approach you can see the castle peering over the roof. This palatial Brain's pub serves the full range of traditional beers from the Cardiff Brewery during the week, though only Brains Dark is on handpump in the wood-panelled public bar on the left. This bar also boasts a rarity for the area: bar billiards. The main lounge offers good food, and the raised part on the right once rang with the words of the preacher Christmas Evans in 1827, before the gospel and the glass parted company.

Suitably refreshed, you should wander up the hill and visit Castell Coch. The building of this fairytale castle in the trees was started in 1875 by the eccentric architect William Burges for the wealthy Lord Bute on the ruins of a 13th-century fortification. Inside its round towers, the medieval fantasy world soars even higher, with extravagantly painted vaulted ceilings. It must be seen to be believed.

Back down the hill in the real world, drop into the ▮**Old Ton Inn (2)**▮ opposite the Lewis Arms. This Whitbread house offers a small range of handpumped beers including Wadworth 6X and Marston's Pedigree. There is a comfortable lounge on the left and a popular bar with a pool table on the right. It also has a beer garden and a skittle alley.

Above: Old Ton Inn.

Pull back on your walking boots for a half-hour trek across the valley. Continue on Merthyr Road to the main roundabout above the A470, next to a sheer rock face. With the old stone bridge on your left, go left across the River Taff and turn right at the next roundabout, going towards Pentyrch. Busy roads now dominate this narrow pass, but note the tall pillars of a former railway viaduct. Pass a few roads to the right and, just before the road goes sharply uphill, turn right to Gwaelod-y-Garth.

Follow the narrow road beneath the hill until you reach the ▮**Gwaelod-y-Garth Inn (3)**▮ on the left. It's tempting just to sit outside on the benches and enjoy the fine views back across the valley, but it's worth venturing inside to see a remarkable wooden price list to the left of the bar. It advertises Fernvale ale at 1s 1d a pint along with Watney's at 1s 8d, plus Webbs bottled beers. All have now vanished, but you can still buy Hancock HB and the odd guest beer for a slightly higher price. There are also old water jugs hanging from the beams and a pool table in the saloon to the right.

Retrace your steps slightly down the road and then go down a public footpath marked to the left. Steep steps lead to a footbridge across the river. Follow the path straight past a school to the old road running through Taffs Well. Immediately on your right is the striking black and white ▼ **Taffs Well Inn (4)** ▼. This comfortable house offers hand-pumped Tetley Bitter and Draught Bass. A beer garden behind overlooks a park. Among the park's attractions is the healing well after which the village and pub are named. Like the next two pubs, the Taffs Well has a good food menu.

A short stroll up the road to the left and over the railway line leads to ▼ **Fagin's Ale and Chop House (5)** ▼. Despite being tucked into a small row of terraced houses, this gem of a free house in the hamlet of Glan-y-Llyn offers one of the widest ranges of real ales in the Cardiff area, some served from casks on stillage behind the bar. There are usually 10 to 12 to choose from, including Caledonian Deuchars, 80/-, and IPA, Brains SA, and Courage Directors. There are occasional beer festivals. Food is served in the evenings from Tuesday to Saturday. Note the stone-flagged floor and odd sayings in "Wenglish" chalked on the beams.

Below: *The Anchor.*

If you can drag yourself away, walk back past the Taffs Well Inn and along the Cardiff Road to ▼ **The Anchor (6)** ▼ on the left, close to Taffs Well Station. While you wait for the train back to Cardiff, you can enjoy a final pint of Brain's Bitter, Wadworth 6X, or Marston's Pedigree. Those who have booked could also try the rare delights of the restaurant that offers Mongolian cuisine.

MAP

48

WALSALL

The football team's nickname, the Saddlers, recalls an era when Walsall was the heart of the saddlemaking industry. Today it is much more diversfied in its industries. With an early 13th-century crypt, St. Matthew's Church is the oldest building in the town. Jerome K. Jerome, author of *Three Men in a Boat*, was born here. He was a man who knew his pubs and enjoyed a drink.

This crawl can be covered easily on foot, starting at the railway station in Station Street. Leave the station, turn right along Station Street, then turn right again into Park Street. Continue along Park Street onto the bridge, turn left onto St. Paul's Street, and, at its junction with Bridge Street, turn into Darwall Street. Here you will find the ❚**Imperial (1)**❚, a Weatherspoon pub in a converted cinema. Beware of Dinosaur attack! Confused? Then see for yourself. It is a very impressive renovation with no expense spared. There is the usual Weatherspoon range of beers: Courage Directors, Theakston Best Bitter, and several guests. There is a no music policy and a non-smoking area.

On leaving, turn right along Darwall Street and take the first right into Leicester Street. Continue along to the end, turn left into Lichfield Street, and cross the road to turn right into the narrow Intown Row. Keep right past a parking lot to junction with Lower Rushall Street and find the ❚**Victoria (2)**❚, a two-room pub reminiscent of a 1980s style wine bar. Despite its updated look, this pub dates back to 1848 and was

Below: The Katz as was — now the Victoria.

originally called the Albert and Victoria. More recently it was the Katz. This name was coined by Irish navvies whose slang name for Queen Victoria was "the Cat." It sells ABC Bitter, Greene King Abbot, Marston's Pedigree, and up to three guest beers. This is a very popular pub that serves good value food. Note the former tower brewery at the back, which now forms the living quarters of the pub.

From the Victoria, turn left down Intown Row and carry on to the bottom of the hill onto Lichfield Street. Cross into Hatherton Road and turn right into Lower Forster Street, where you will find the ❦**Fountain (3)**❦, a current *Good Beer Guide* (CAMRA, 1999) entry. It serves Draught Bass, Highgate Mild, and a guest beer. It is a classic two-room pub with a bright saloon bar, a homely small lounge, and a loggia. A very snug and cozy place, it must not be missed, as this sort of pub is rare since pub planners think taking walls out and opening spaces is the "in thing."

Above: The Fountain.

From the Fountain turn right along Lower Forster Street. At the junction of Littleton Street turn left and walk towards the traffic lights, taking the third right into Wisemore and passing the Leather Museum. (The museum is situated in an old leather works and is well worth a visit if you pass during the day.) Continue along Wisemore into Garden Street, then turn left at the end into Portland Street and right along Stafford Street. Turn right on John Street, which will take you to the ❦**Tap and Spile (4)**❦, the 1997 CAMRA local branch Pub of the Year and a regular *Good Beer Guide* entry. It is known locally as the "Pretty Bricks" because of the ceramic tiles on the frontage. The Tap and Spile is a two-room pub with a bright front bar featuring lots of wood and glass. There are eight regularly changing beers, including Highgate Dark, and excellent home-cooked food. There are frequent theme nights — Mexican, Indian, etc. This is a genuine pub where the decor matches the period.

Leave the Tap and Spile and return to Stafford Street. Turn left and pass the law courts on the right. Turn right into Court Way and left into Green Lane for the ❦**Oak (5)**❦. It is a regular *Good Beer Guide* entry and more than a century old. This one-room pub has an unusual island bar. Courage Best Bitter and four or five frequently changing guest beers are sold along with good value food. The pub is vibrant in the evenings and busy with office and factory workers at lunch-time. It's a friendly local offering a warm welcome to all.

Turn left along Green Lane then right at the end into Wolverhampton Street, where you'll face the ▼**Wharf (6)**▼. This brand new pub, built and owned by Highgate Brewery, opened in December 1997. It features acres of glass facing the canal wharf. With a totally wooden interior, it could almost be in Sweden! Highgate's decision to build a brand new pub without any period parody caused some gasps when it was unveiled. It is not to everyone's taste architecturally, but it was named Best New Pub in Britain in the English Heritage/CAMRA awards. A full range of Highgate beers is available along with good food, including breakfast (available from 8 A.M). Live music and comedy nights are held regularly.

Leave the Wharf and continue back along Wolverhampton Street, past Woolworths and back into Park Street. The *Red Lion* on the right is worth a look. To get the best view, stand on the other side of the pedestrian area and look up to see the stone lion guarding the pub. An ongoing fight of 20 years by CAMRA and some keen local councillors eventually persuaded the town planners to build the new shops around the pub. Pass the Red Lion, turn right into Station Street, and head back to the railway station.

49

WHARFEDALE

This pleasant circular ramble through Upper Wharfedale links four charming pubs and can be either five miles or seven miles long. It is essentially a summer walk, particularly if you use the bus services up the valley, for out of season they are, to say the least, irregular. In addition to the pubs, it takes in a delightful riverside walk, much of it on the Dales Way; lots of interesting wild life; and some spectacular views. Information on bus services can be obtained from Keighley and District Transport. School bus services also take other passengers. It is best to plan this route carefully, bearing in mind the opening hours of the pubs.

The best starting point is in Starbotton at the **❦Fox and Hounds (1)❦**, a welcoming village inn with low beams,

flagged floors, and open fires. It serves above average, good value pub food, including vegetarian choices. It also provides bed and breakfast accommodations. Handpumped beers include Taylor Landlord, Theakston Best Bitter and Old Peculier, and Black Sheep Best with guest beers during the summer months. In summer it closes during the afternoons and on Monday evenings. In winter it is best to check its availability by phoning. The pub has a sizeable parking lot, but one needs to seek the approval of the landlord to use it while walking out from there.

Above: *Fox and Hounds.*

Turn left on the main road towards Kettlewell, and three hundred yards along on your right is a footpath sign to Buckden. Go down a disused cart track and cross the River Wharfe by a footbridge, then turn right and follow the river bank for five hundred yards. The path then leaves the river and goes through meadows and alongside Firth Woods. In spring and summer there are many varieties of birds along this stretch, and walkers have been rewarded by sightings of buzzards and more common birds such as curlews, mallards, shovellers, and dippers. At Birks Wood the path rejoins the river, and it is a flat, easy walk to the bridge at Buckden. At this point you have a choice of routes: turning left and using the road or crossing the

Above: *The George.*

road and continuing to follow the footpath by the river. Both routes lead to Hubberholme.

The next pub is ❦**The George (2)**❦, which nestles at the foot of the hills by the bridge. This 18th-century white-washed pub comes as a welcome haven after the first hour's walk. In its early days it was a farmhouse and later the vicarage for St. Michael's Church across the bridge. Pub, church, and bridge form Yorkshire's smallest conservation area. Beers include Black Sheep Special, Theakston Black Bull, and Younger's Scotch Bitter. The pub still retains its stone-flagged floors, open fires, and mullion windows. There are five letting bedrooms. The blackboard menu has English, Thai, and vegetarian dishes and homemade pies and soups. The pub closes in the afternoon.

Take time to visit the beautiful Norman church and view the memorial to Yorkshire's most famous author, J. B. Priestley, who claimed the George as his favorite pub. The church has the only rood loft in the former West Riding, and the stalls were built by "Mousey" Thompson of Kilburn.

Now follow the road on the north side of the river and, just before a road junction, take the footpath. It's a stiff climb up Cray Gill, with views of the waterfalls on the left. You soon arrive in Cray at the ❦**White Lion (3)**❦, a 17th-century inn, the highest in Wharfedale. It was previously used by packhorse traders and drovers taking their cattle to markets in the midlands and London. Walkers are welcome here, but you are expected to take off any muddy boots before entering. There is an open fire and stone-flagged floors, and the walls are covered with old farming implements. The interesting old game of Ring the Bull is played here. The beers are Moorhouse Premier and Pendle Witch, Tetley Bitter, and occasional guests.

There are some sophisticated dishes on the menu and lots of good plain food, including casseroles and large Yorkshire puddings with various fillings. The pub is open all day in summer but closes during the afternoon in winter. Bed and breakfast accommodation is available; there may be price breaks in the winter.

Above: *The Buck Inn.*

From the White Lion cross the road and the stream by the stepping stones and follow the footpath signs for Buckden. There is a short, sharp climb to join the ridge path, which turns right along a well-defined track that drops through Rakes Wood and ends up in Buckden parking lot. From the ridge the views over Upper Wharfedale are magnificent.

Cross the parking lot to ❚**The Buck Inn (4)**❚, a splendid stone-faced country inn that faces the sloping village green. It was here at Christmas in 1945 that Denis and Edna (now Lord and Lady) Healey spent their honeymoon in the loft of an adjoining barn. Today there is plenty of room at the inn. There is a restaurant and bar, open fires, and comfortable seating. On sale are a full range of Theakston ales and occasional guest beers. There is a bar food menu and a full restaurant service including morning coffee and afternoon tea. The bar is open all day.

If you have travelled by bus from the Skipton direction it is possible to end the ramble here and return south. Or you can continue a further two miles along the main road back to Starbotton. The flexibility of this crawl is entirely with the walker. Read it as you wish, but enjoy it.

50

YORK

York is the most civilized of places and has a lot going for it in history, architecture, and culture. And it has some great pubs. This crawl takes in seven of them, with a brief glance at three others. It crosses the river twice, skirts the great Minster, goes through the famous walls, visits two very interesting churches, and concludes with a stroll through a delightful park. So let's go.

We start at ❦**The Maltings (1)**❦ in Tanners Moat, which is close to both the railway station and the bus terminus in Rogier Street. It was originally named the Railway Tavern and was probably built to serve the newly opened station. Later it was called the Lendal Bridge.

It is a small, higgledy piggledy sort of pub — just one main room with a side private room, or "snug," — but it is blessed with loads of character and characters. Someone with a sense of humor has been at work here: the walls are lined with old doors and wood panels and there are metal signs aplenty. Sean Collinge runs the place with some style, and his selection of beers cannot be faulted. Black Sheep is a regular along with one of the Rooster selection and often one from the nearby York brewery. Others generally come from local micros, of which there are many in Yorkshire, along with the excellent Budweiser Budwar and Leffe Blond on draught. Food, substantial and well priced, is available at lunchtime every day of the week. York CAMRA chose it as its Pub of the Year in 1996.

"The antiquity of York...showed itself so visably at a distance that we could not but observe it before we came quite up to the city..."

Daniel Defoe

Walk to the right across Lendal Bridge and view the Guildhall and some of the other splendid buildings on the opposite side of the river. The first one across the bridge is the former York Club, which is now an Italian restaurant. Turn right into Lendal, and on the right, next to the Mansion House and in cellars under the main Post Office, is the ❦**Lendal Cellars (2)**❦. It is a Whitbread Hogshead alehouse with a wide variety of beers, including some from Bateman, Marston's Head Brewer's Choice, and local independents as well as Whitbread beers. It has newspapers to read and a good menu. It is spacious, but when it fills up with young people in the evenings, it gets rather noisy.

Follow your nose down Stonegate towards York Minster, and on the right is the ❦**Punch Bowl (3)**❦, recognized by its impressive frontage of carved bargeboards that date from 1675 and a Hammond's Tower Brewery plaque. There are three rooms in this Bass pub and a good choice of beers from the company's portfolio, plus guests. The food is good, with an accent on midday catering to visitors.

Further along Stonegate, the next stop is easily recognized by the rare gallows sign spanning the street. ❦**The Olde Starre Inn (4)**❦ is tucked away down an alley on the left. It is one of York's oldest inns, with parts dating back to the 14th century. It's possibly also the most haunted establishment, with at least four different spectres, for the building was used as a hospital during the Civil War. Freakish occurrences include screams from soldiers being amputated without the benefit of anaesthetic. The bar is in a basic lounge, although there are two comfortable snugs. A former owner, Brett Brothers, is depicted in a splendid glazed bar screen. There is also a dining area and a courtyard. A selection of Theakston beers is on sale, and there is a wide range of food available.

After leaving Stonegate turn left and take the time to visit the oddly placed little church on your right. This is St. Michael-le-Belfrey, which has its origins in the 11th century and was originally a chapel of ease for the Minster. It now exists in its own right as a parish church. It has a beautiful reredos, a handsome gallery, and some wonderful 14th-century stained glass.

Below: York Arms.

Next stop is the ❦**York Arms (5)**❦ on High Petergate, a neighbor of the Minster. It is in the usual neat and tidy style of Sam Smith, and there are two entrances. The one on the right leads to a tiny snug, accessed by a sliding door, in which locals hold sway. It leads on to a larger, comfortable lounge. The left door opens to a large, airy room with lots of interest, including a wonderful photograph of the Minster taken by Barry Grayson, a former and very popular landlord. There are some great tales of hauntings in this pub — ask the locals. Old Brewery Bitter is, naturally, the only draught beer, but Sam's produces some fine bottled beers that are worth trying. Food is available at most times, and there are also rooms to let.

Carry on in the same direction and go under the famous walls at Bootham Bar, crossing the busy junction at Gillygate into Bootham. Visit the splendidly unspoiled ❦**Bootham Tavern (6)**❦, a pub that has remained unchanged for many years and uncompromising in its purpose. The taproom is airy, basic, and friendly; it hosts an old embossed sign for Tetley beers and a hoist once used for lifting casks in and out of the cellar. The smallish lounge is darker, a tad more comfortable, and is where visitors who make it this far out of the city walls will drink. Tetley Bitter, always in excellent form, is the only draught beer on sale. Food and drink are pretty simple, but this pub is a must.

Cross the road again and take care, for it's very busy here due to folks thinking they will be able to park in the city center. They won't. A word of advice here for anyone driving to York is to use the excellent Park and Ride system, which offers three large, free parking lots on the outskirts of the city and a cheap bus service into the center.

On the corner of Marygate is a semicircular projection, St. Mary's Tower, which was once the repository of the records of Yorkshire monasteries and is part of the walls of St. Mary's Abbey. when it was mined during the Civil War, bang! went the records. The rebuilding was on a smaller scale. Just around the corner is a splendid view of the Minster, framed incongruously by a bowling green.

Marygate contains many handsome Georgian and Victorian buildings, not least of which is the ❦**Minster Inn (7)**❦, a little bit out of the period, for it was built in 1903 for the Tadcaster Tower Brewery. It has a simple layout with a corridor bar that

Above: *Minster Inn.*

also serves the taproom, two enclosed rooms, a smoke room, and what was originally intended as a coffee room. This delightful former Bass pub now belongs to one of the burgeoning pub groups and has Draught Bass and John Smith Bitter as regulars along with two guests, often not very inspired choices such as Morland Old Speckled Hen and Theakston Best Bitter. Food is pretty simple, just rather good sandwiches. Its eponymous neighbor is often used as an excuse for a Sunday lunchtime drink: "Just off to the Minster dear, won't be long."

It's time now, appropriately, for a little more spiritual refreshment. Cross Marygate, head towards the river, and call in at St. Olave's Church. Its origins are 11th century, but most of it is an 18th-century rebuild. Among many items of interest is a rest for a wooden leg in the third pew from the front. On leaving the church enter St. Mary's Gardens through the Abbey gatehouse. On the left are the ruins of the abbey, and next to this is the Yorkshire Museum. The path leads you back into Museum Street. Cross the bridge and you are back where you started, so why not try another pint at the Maltings? A good idea. Cheers!

MAP SECTION

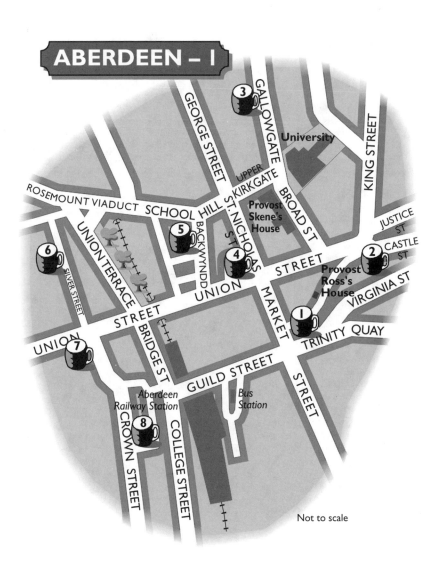

ABERDEEN – 1

University

GEORGE STREET

GALLOWGATE

KING STREET

UPPER KIRKGATE

Provost Skene's House

ROSEMOUNT VIADUCT

SCHOOL HILL

ST. NICHOLAS ST

BROAD ST

JUSTICE ST

CASTLE ST

UNION TERRACE

BACKWYNND ST

UNION

STREET

Provost Ross's House

VIRGINIA ST

SILVER STREET

STREET

MARKET

TRINITY QUAY

BRIDGE ST

STREET

UNION

GUILD STREET

STREET

Aberdeen Railway Station

Bus Station

CROWN STREET

COLLEGE STREET

Not to scale

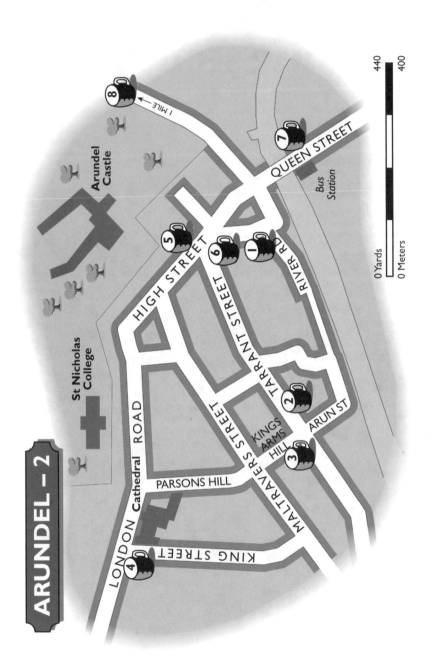

ARUNDEL – 2

Arundel Castle

St Nicholas College

HIGH STREET

London Cathedral ROAD

PARSONS HILL

KING STREET

MALTRAVERS STREET

KINGS ARMS HILL

TARRANT STREET

ARUN ST

RIVER R

QUEEN STREET

Bus Station

1 MILE

0 Yards 440
0 Meters 400

176

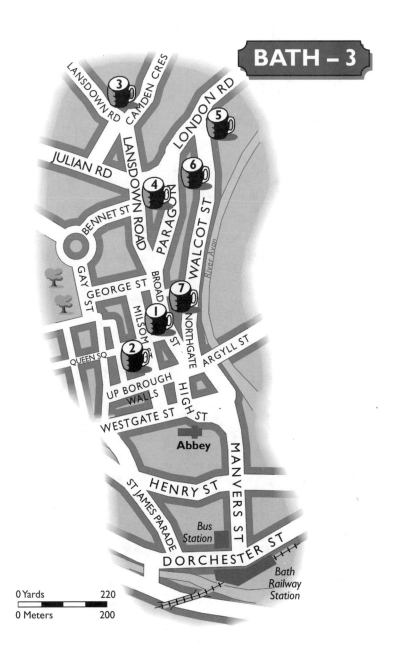

BATH – 3

LANSDOWN RD
CAMDEN CRES
3
LONDON RD
5
JULIAN RD
LANSDOWN ROAD
6
4
PARAGON
BENNET ST
WALCOT ST
River Avon
GAY ST
GEORGE ST
BROAD ST
7
MILSOM ST
1
NORTHGATE
QUEEN SQ
2
ARGYLL ST
UP BOROUGH WALLS
HIGH ST
WESTGATE ST
Abbey
MANVERS ST
HENRY ST
ST JAMES PARADE
Bus Station
DORCHESTER ST
Bath Railway Station

0 Yards 220
0 Meters 200

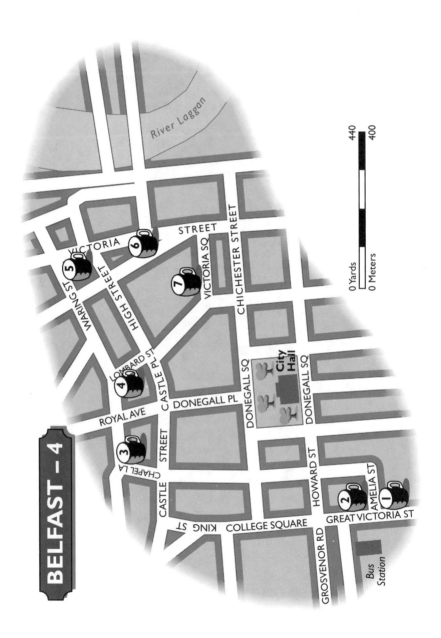

BELFAST – 4

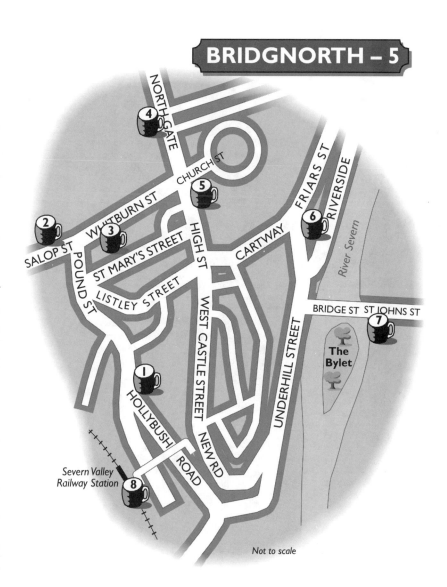

BRIDGNORTH – 5

NORTHGATE

CHURCH ST

WHITBURN ST

SALOP ST

POUND ST

ST MARY'S STREET

LISTLEY STREET

HIGH ST

WEST CASTLE STREET

CARTWAY

FRIARS ST

RIVERSIDE

River Severn

BRIDGE ST

ST JOHNS ST

UNDERHILL STREET

The Bylet

HOLLYBUSH ROAD

NEW RD

Severn Valley
Railway Station

Not to scale

179

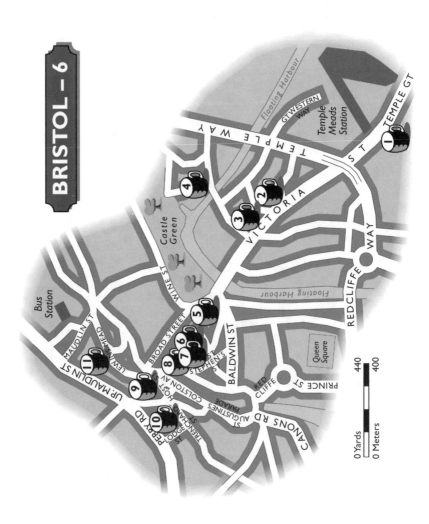

BRISTOL – 6

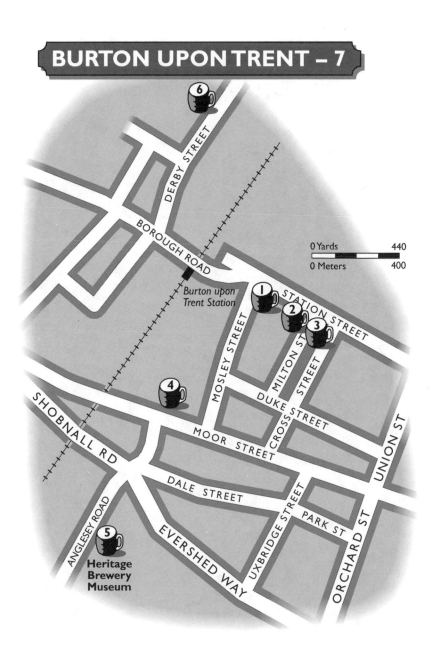

0 Yards 440
0 Meters 400

Burton upon
Trent Station

DERBY STREET

BOROUGH ROAD

STATION STREET

MOSLEY STREET

MILTON ST

CROSS STREET

DUKE STREET

MOOR STREET

SHOBNALL RD

DALE STREET

UXBRIDGE STREET

PARK ST

ORCHARD ST

UNION ST

EVERSHED WAY

ANGLESEY ROAD

Heritage
Brewery
Museum

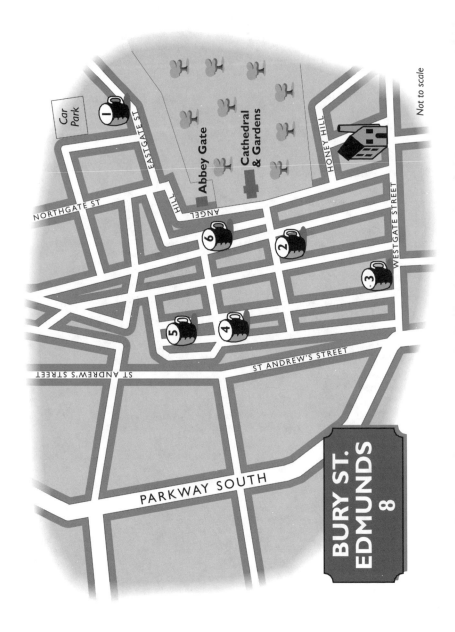

Car Park

EASTGATE ST

NORTHGATE ST

Abbey Gate

ANGEL HILL

Cathedral & Gardens

HONEY HILL

WEST GATE STREET

ST ANDREW'S STREET

ST ANDREW'S STREET

PARKWAY SOUTH

Not to scale

BURY ST. EDMUNDS
8

182

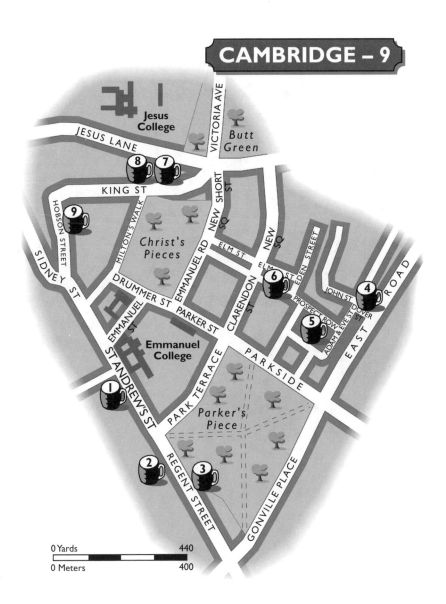

Jesus College

JESUS LANE

Butt Green

VICTORIA AVE

8 7

KING ST

NEW SHORT ST

HOBSON STREET

9

MILTON'S WALK

Christ's Pieces

EMMANUEL RD

ELM ST

NEW SQ

EDEN STREET

SIDNEY ST

DRUMMER ST

PARKER ST

CLARENDON ST

ELM ST

6

PROSPECT ROW

JOHN ST

DOVER ST

EAST ROAD

4

5

ADAM & EVE ST

EMMANUEL ST

Emmanuel College

PARK TERRACE

PARKSIDE

ST ANDREW'S ST

1

Parker's Piece

2

REGENT STREET

3

GONVILLE PLACE

0 Yards 440
0 Meters 400

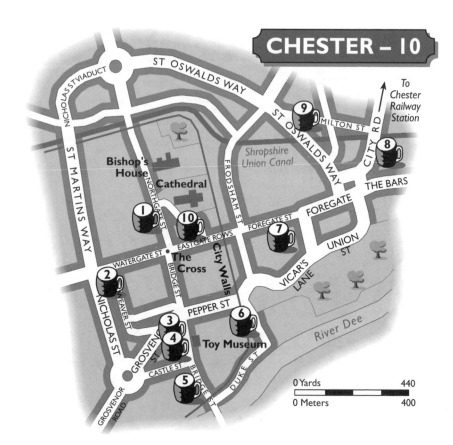

CHESTER – 10

St Oswalds Way

Nicholas St Viaduct

St Martins Way

St Oswalds Way

Milton St

City Rd

To Chester Railway Station

Bishop's House

Cathedral

Shropshire Union Canal

Frodsham St

Foregate St

The Bars

Foregate

North Gate St

Eastgate Rows

Watergate St

The Cross

City Walls

Foregate St

Union St

Vicar's Lane

River Dee

Nicholas St

Weaver St

Bridge St

Pepper St

Grosvenor

Castle St

Toy Museum

Duke St

Bridge St

Grosvenor Road

0 Yards   440
0 Meters   400

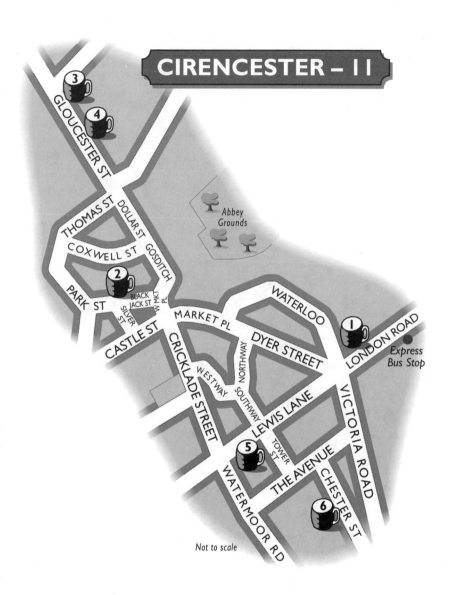

CIRENCESTER – 11

Abbey Grounds

GLOUCESTER ST

THOMAS ST

DOLLAR ST

GOSDITCH

COXWELL ST

PARK ST

BLACK JACK ST

SILVER ST

W MKT PL

CASTLE ST

MARKET PL

CRICKLADE STREET

WESTWAY

SOUTHWAY

NORTHWAY

WATERLOO

DYER STREET

LEWIS LANE

TOWER ST

WATERMOOR RD

THE AVENUE

CHESTER ST

VICTORIA ROAD

LONDON ROAD

Express
Bus Stop

Not to scale

185

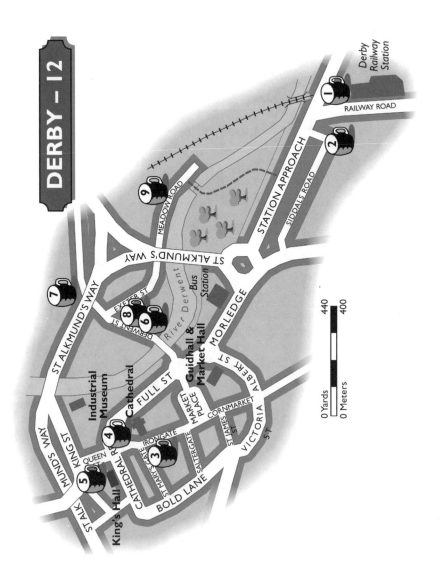

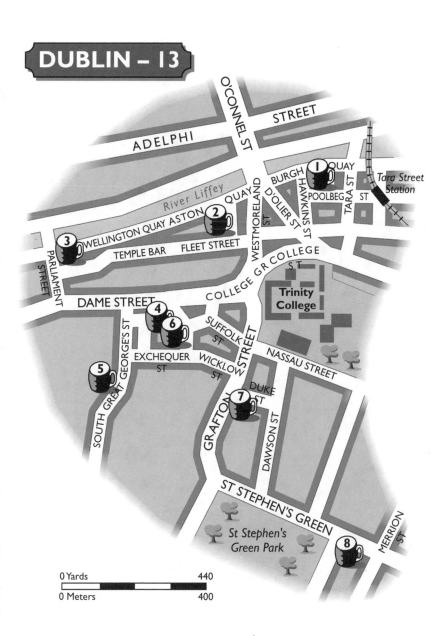

DUBLIN – 13

O'CONNELL STREET

ADELPHI ST

O'CONNELL ST

River Liffey

WELLINGTON QUAY

ASTON QUAY

D'OLIER ST

WESTMORELAND ST

BURGH QUAY

HAWKINS ST

POOLBEG ST

TARA ST

QUAY

Tara Street Station

TEMPLE BAR

FLEET STREET

PARLIAMENT STREET

DAME STREET

COLLEGE GR

COLLEGE ST

Trinity College

SOUTH GREAT GEORGE'S ST

EXCHEQUER ST

WICKLOW ST

SUFFOLK ST

COLLEGE STREET

NASSAU STREET

GRAFTON STREET

DUKE ST

DAWSON ST

ST STEPHEN'S GREEN

St Stephen's Green Park

MERRION ST

0 Yards	440
0 Meters	400

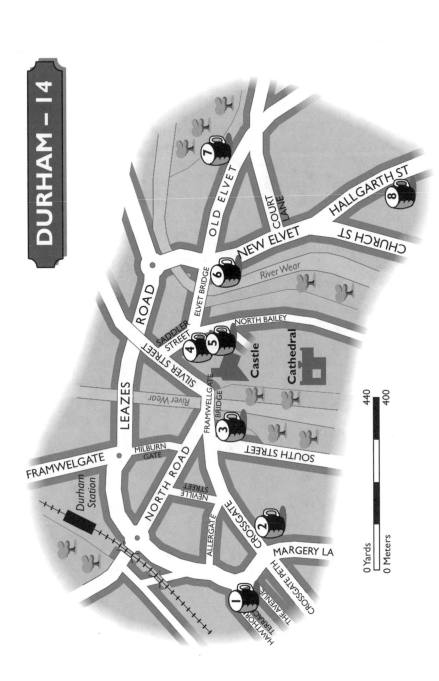

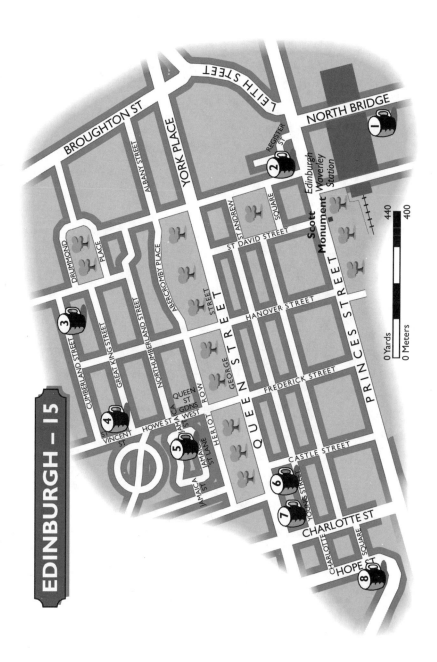

EDINBURGH – 15

BROUGHTON ST

YORK PLACE

LEITH STREET

NORTH BRIDGE

ALBANY STREET

REGISTER ST

Edinburgh
Waverley
Station

Scott
Monument

DRUMMOND PLACE

ABERCROMBY PLACE

ST ANDREW SQUARE

ST DAVID STREET

ST ANDREW STREET

NORTHUMBERLAND STREET

GREAT KING STREET

CUMBERLAND STREET

HANOVER STREET

PRINCES STREET

GEORGE STREET

QUEEN STREET

FREDERICK STREET

HERIOT ROW

QUEEN ST GDNS WEST

HOWE ST

JAMAICA ST

JAMAICA ST LANE

CASTLE STREET

YOUNG STREET

CHARLOTTE ST

CHARLOTTE SQUARE

HOPE ST

S VINCENT ST

0 Yards   440

0 Meters   400

189

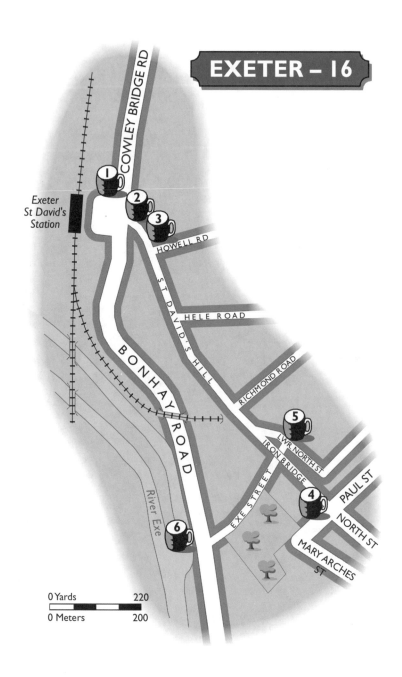

EXETER – 16

Exeter
St David's
Station

COWLEY BRIDGE RD

HOWELL RD

ST DAVID'S HILL

HELE ROAD

RICHMOND ROAD

BONHAY ROAD

River Exe

LWR NORTH ST

IRON BRIDGE

EXE STREET

PAUL ST

NORTH ST

MARY ARCHES
ST

0 Yards 220
0 Meters 200

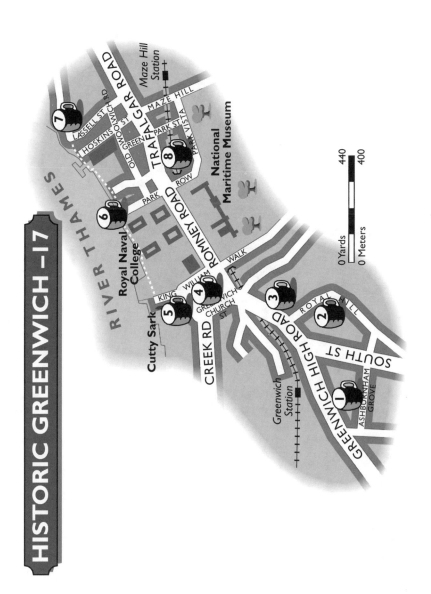

HISTORIC GREENWICH -17

RIVER THAMES

TRAFALGAR ROAD

LASSELL ST RD

HOSKINS ST

OLD WOOLWICH RD

GREENWICH

Maze Hill
Station

MAZE HILL

Park St

PARK VISTA

National
Maritime Museum

Royal Naval
College

Park
ROW

ROMNEY ROAD

WALK

Cutty Sark

KING
WILLIAM

GREENWICH
CHURCH
ST

CREEK RD

ROYAL HILL

GREENWICH HIGH ROAD

SOUTH ST

ASHBURNHAM
GROVE

Greenwich
Station

0 Yards   440

0 Meters   400

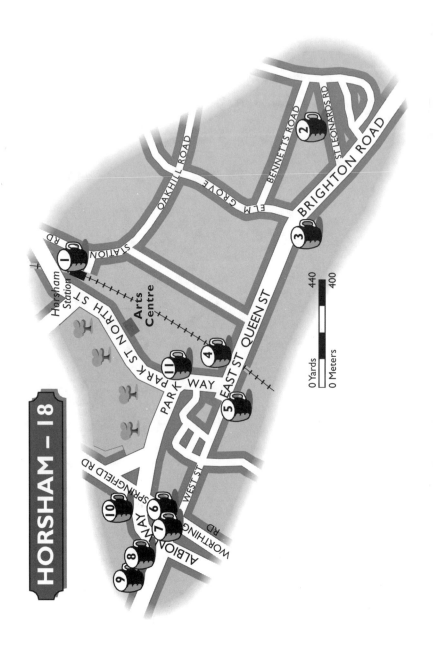

HORSHAM – 18

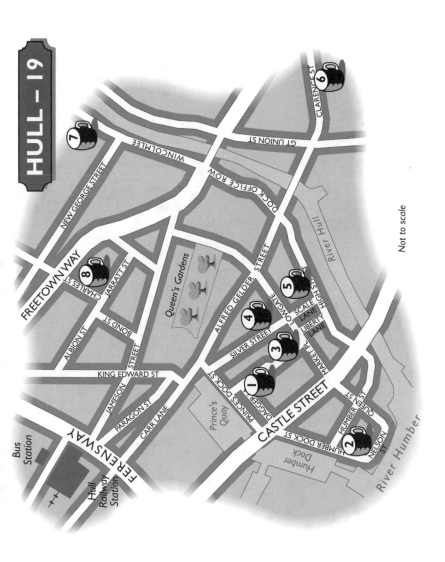

HULL – 19

Not to scale

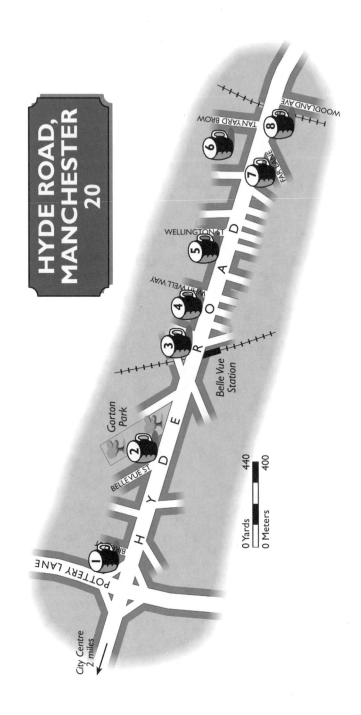

HYDE ROAD, MANCHESTER
20

POTTERY LANE

City Centre
2 miles

HYDE ROAD

BIRCH ST

BELLEVUE ST

Gorton
Park

Belle Vue
Station

WELLWELL WAY

WELLINGTON ST

FAR LANE

TAN YARD BROW

WOODLAND AVE

0 Yards   440
0 Meters   400

KENDAL – 21

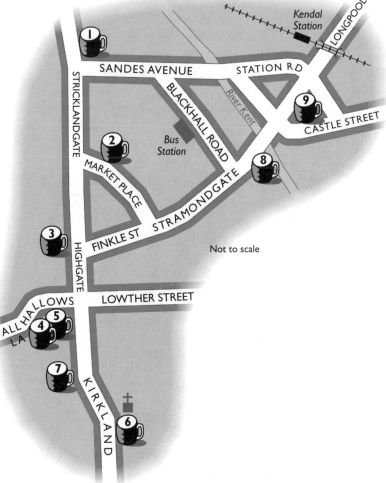

Kendal Station

LONGPOOL

SANDES AVENUE   STATION RD

STRICKLANDGATE

BLACKHALL ROAD

River Kent

CASTLE STREET

Bus Station

MARKET PLACE

STRAMONDGATE

FINKLE ST

Not to scale

HIGHGATE

LOWTHER STREET

ALL HALLOWS

LA

KIRKLAND

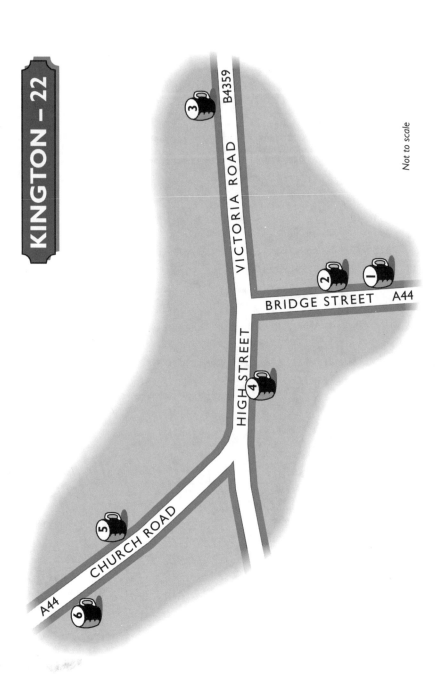

KINGTON – 22

Not to scale

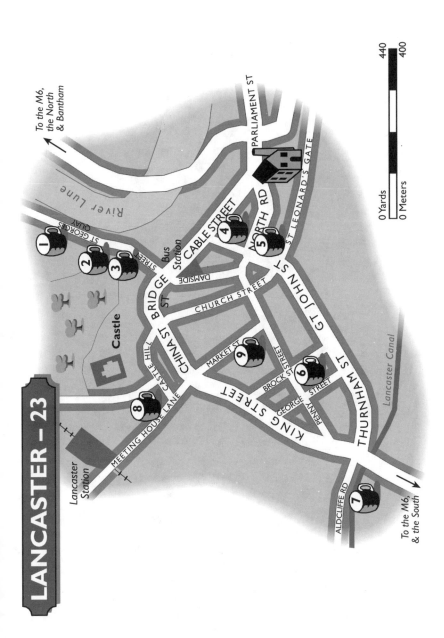

LANCASTER – 23

To the M6,
the North
& Bantham

River Lune

ST GEORGE'S QUAY

Castle

Lancaster
Station

PARLIAMENT ST

NORTH RD

ST LEONARD'S GATE

CABLE STREET

DAMSIDE

Bus
Station

BRIDGE ST

CHURCH STREET

GT JOHN ST

Lancaster Canal

CHINA ST

CASTLE HILL

MEETING HOUSE LANE

MARKET ST

BROCK STREET

GEORGE STREET

PENNY STREET

KING STREET

THURNHAM ST

ALDCLIFFE RD

To the M6,
& the South

0 Yards   440

0 Meters   400

LEDBURY – 24

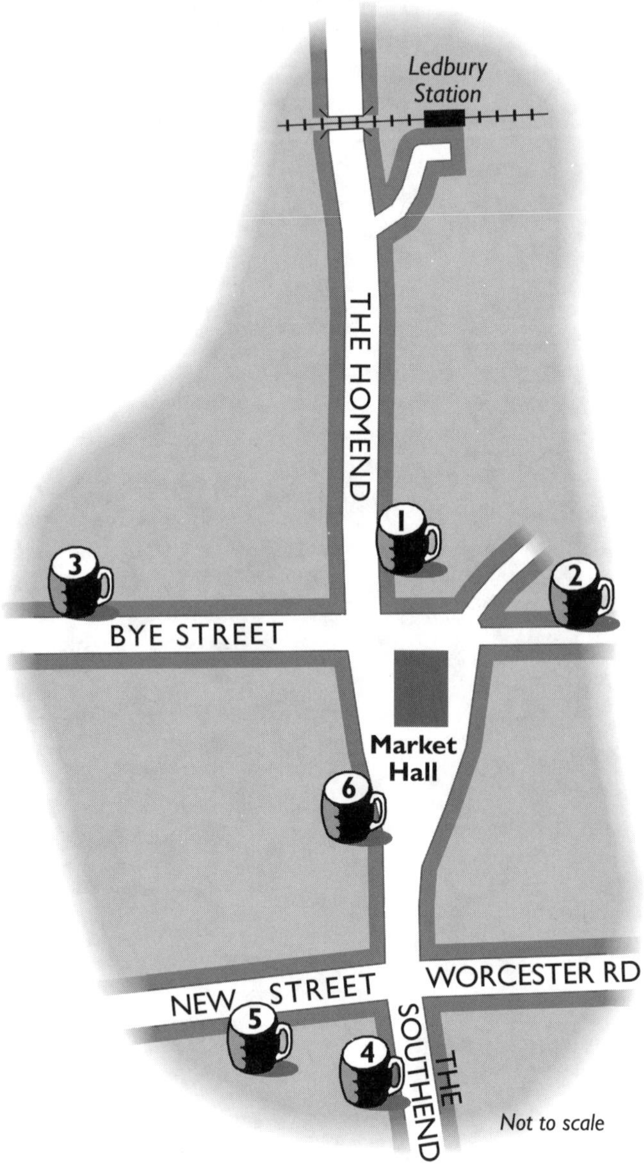

Ledbury Station

THE HOMEND

BYE STREET

Market Hall

WORCESTER RD

NEW STREET

THE SOUTHEND

Not to scale

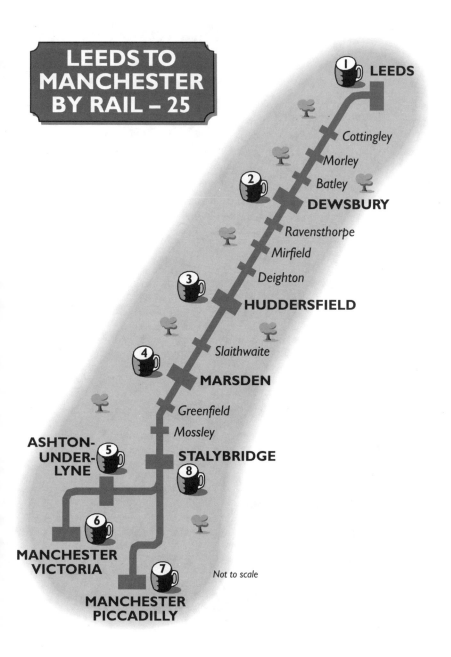

LEEDS TO MANCHESTER BY RAIL – 25

1 LEEDS

Cottingley
Morley
Batley

2 DEWSBURY

Ravensthorpe
Mirfield
Deighton

3 HUDDERSFIELD

Slaithwaite

4 MARSDEN

Greenfield
Mossley

ASHTON-UNDER-LYNE 5

STALYBRIDGE

8

6 MANCHESTER VICTORIA

7 MANCHESTER PICCADILLY

Not to scale

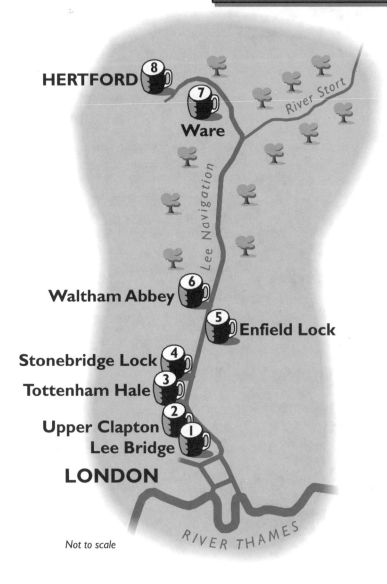

LEE VALLEY
BY BOAT – 26

HERTFORD 8

7

Ware

River Stort

Lee Navigation

Waltham Abbey 6

5 Enfield Lock

Stonebridge Lock 4

Tottenham Hale 3

Upper Clapton 2

Lee Bridge 1

LONDON

RIVER THAMES

Not to scale

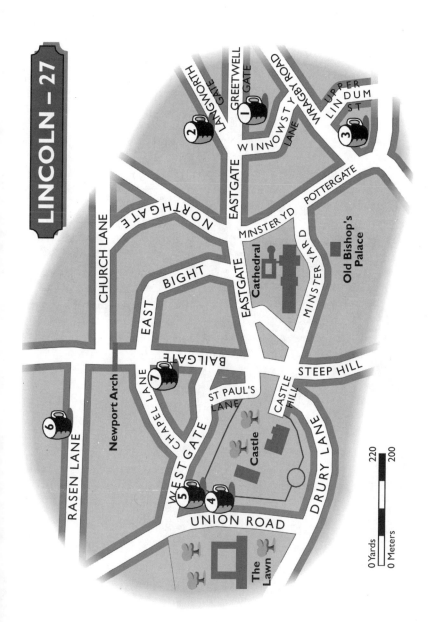

Old Bishop's Palace

Cathedral

Castle

The Lawn

Newport Arch

GREETWELL GATE

LANGWORTH GATE

WINNOWSTY LANE

WRAGBY ROAD

UPPER LINDUM ST

EASTGATE

POTTERGATE

MINSTER YD

MINSTER YARD

NORTHGATE

CHURCH LANE

EAST BIGHT

EASTGATE

BAILGATE

STEEP HILL

ST PAUL'S LANE

CASTLE HILL

CHAPEL LANE

WEST GATE

RASEN LANE

UNION ROAD

DRURY LANE

0 Yards   220

0 Meters   200

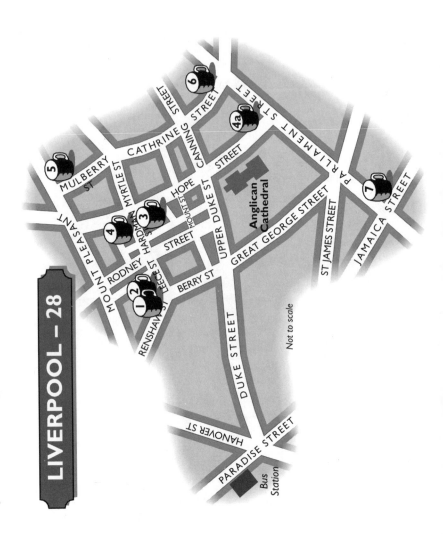

LIVERPOOL – 28

CATHRINE STREET

CANNING STREET

MULBERRY ST

MYRTLE ST

MOUNT PLEASANT

HARDMAN ST

RODNEY ST

LEECE ST

RENSHAW ST

HOPE STREET

MOUNT ST

UPPER DUKE ST

BERRY ST

DUKE STREET

HANOVER ST

PARADISE STREET

PARLIAMENT STREET

GREAT GEORGE STREET

ST JAMES STREET

JAMAICA STREET

Anglican Cathedral

Bus Station

Not to scale

1
2
3
4
4a
5
6
7

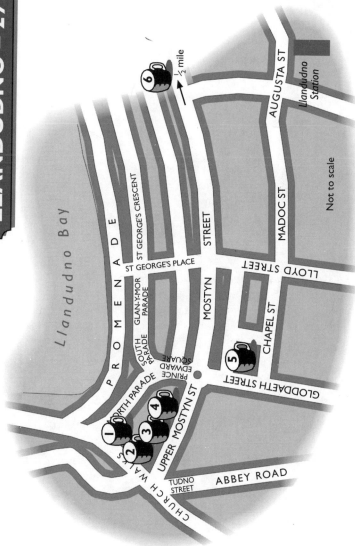

LLANDUDNO – 29

Llandudno Bay

PROMENADE

ST GEORGE'S CRESCENT
ST GEORGE'S PLACE
GLAN-Y-MOR PARADE
SOUTH PARADE
NORTH PARADE
CHURCH WALKS
PRINCE EDWARD SQUARE
UPPER MOSTYN ST
MOSTYN STREET
CHAPEL ST
GLODDAETH STREET
TUDNO STREET
ABBEY ROAD
AUGUSTA ST
MADOC ST
LLOYD STREET

Llandudno Station

Not to scale

½ mile

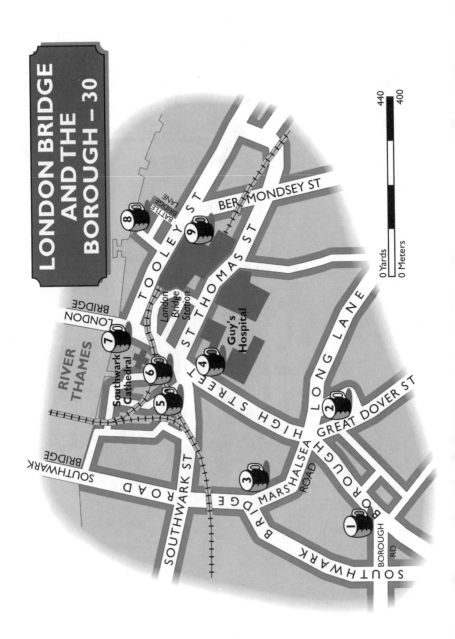

LONDON BRIDGE
AND THE
BOROUGH – 30

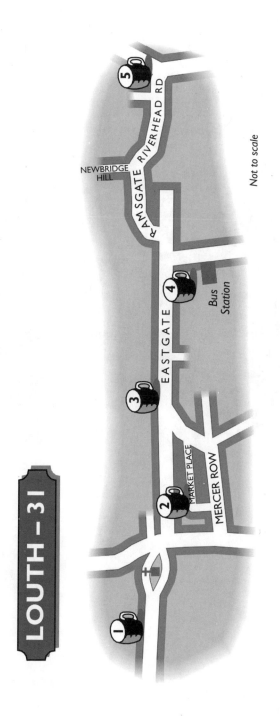

LOUTH – 31

NEWBRIDGE
HILL

RAMSGATE RIVERHEAD RD

EASTGATE

MARKET PLACE

MERCER ROW

Bus
Station

Not to scale

1

2

3

4

5

South
Wimbledon

Colliers
Wood

QUICKS ROAD

ALL SAINTS RD

MERTON RD

HAYDONS ROAD

NORMAN RD

DE BURGH RD

COLLIERS WOOD

HIGH ST

Colliers
Wood

PRIORY
ROAD

KINGSTON RD

MERTON HIGH STREET

PINCOTT RD

ABBEY RD

HIGH PATH

CHRISTCHURCH ROAD

MERANTUM WAY

MORDEN ROAD

DORSET ROAD

Morden
Road
Station

**MERTON &
SOUTH WIMBLEDON
32**

0 Yards   440

0 Meters   400

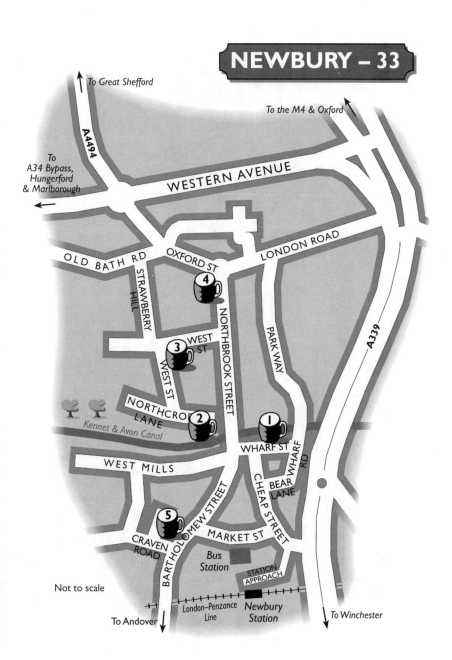

To Great Shefford

To the M4 & Oxford

To
A34 Bypass,
Hungerford
& Marlborough

A4494

WESTERN AVENUE

OLD BATH RD

OXFORD ST

LONDON ROAD

STRAWBERRY HILL

4

NORTHBROOK STREET

PARK WAY

A339

3 WEST ST

WEST ST

NORTHCROFT LANE

2

1

Kennet & Avon Canal

WHARF ST

WHARF RD

WEST MILLS

BEAR LANE

BARTHOLOMEW STREET

CHEAP STREET

5

CRAVEN ROAD

MARKET ST

Bus Station

STATION APPROACH

Not to scale

London–Penzance Line

Newbury Station

To Andover

To Winchester

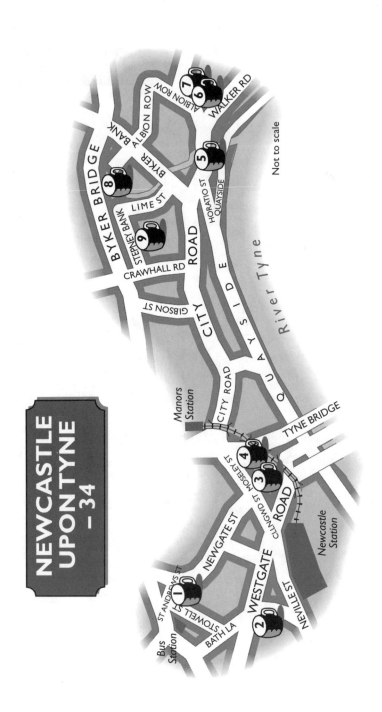

NEWCASTLE
UPON TYNE
– 34

Not to scale

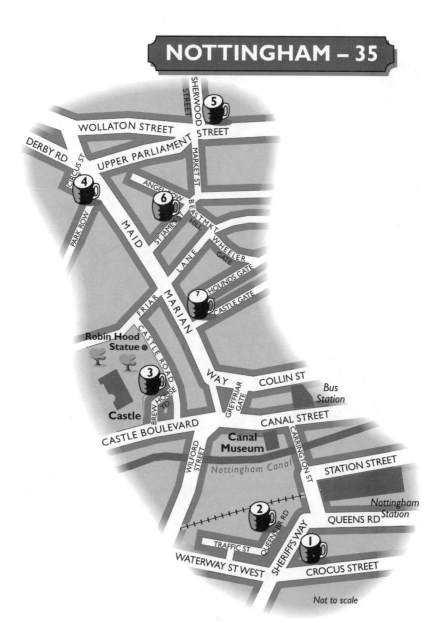

NOTTINGHAM – 35

WOLLATON STREET

DERBY RD

CIRCUS ST

UPPER PARLIAMENT

SHERWOOD STREET

STREET

MARKET ST

5

4

PARK ROW

MAID

ANGEL ROW

ST JAMES ST

6

BEASTMKT HILL

WHEELER GATE

FRIAR LANE

MARIAN

7

HOUNDS GATE

CASTLE GATE

Robin Hood Statue

CASTLE ROAD

WAY

GREYFRIAR GATE

COLLIN ST

Bus Station

Castle

3

BREW HOUSE YD

CASTLE BOULEVARD

WILFORD STREET

Canal Museum

CANAL STREET

CARRINGTON ST

STATION STREET

Nottingham Canal

QUEENS BR. RD

2

SHERIFFS WAY

QUEENS RD

Nottingham Station

TRAFFIC ST

WATERWAY ST WEST

1

CROCUS STREET

Not to scale

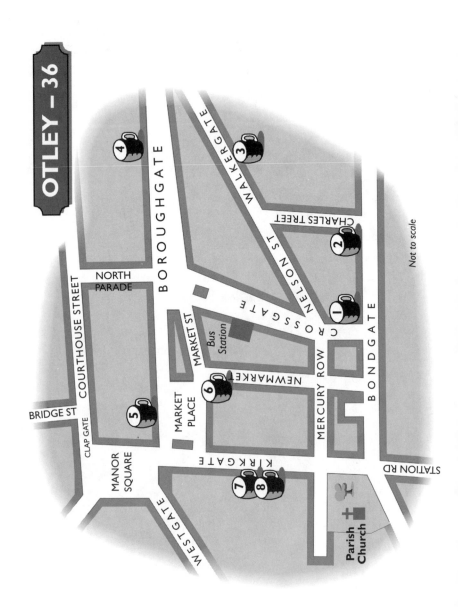

Not to scale

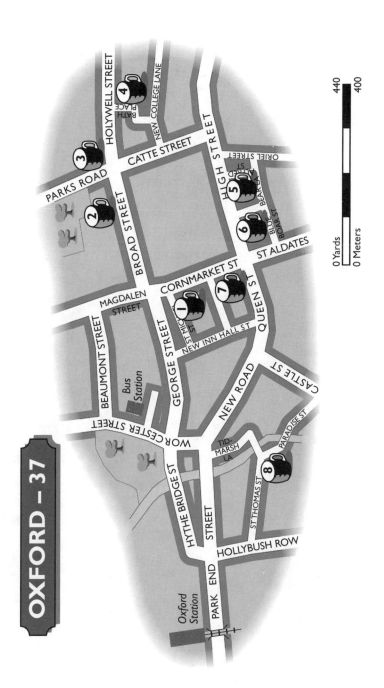

OXFORD – 37

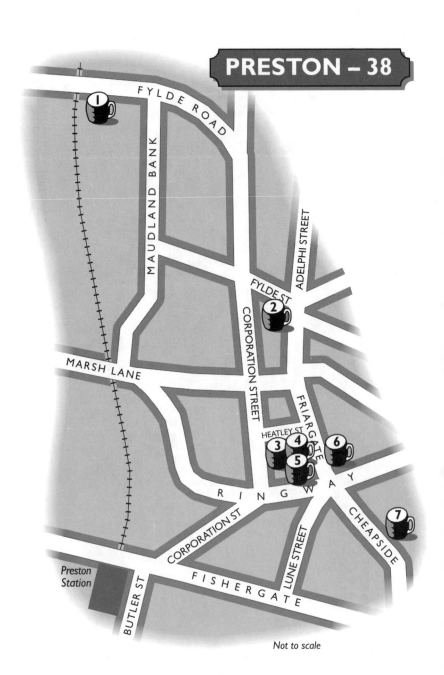

PRESTON – 38

FYLDE ROAD

MAUDLAND BANK

ADELPHI STREET

FYLDE ST

CORPORATION STREET

MARSH LANE

FRIARGATE

HEATLEY ST

R I N G W A Y

CORPORATION ST

CHEAPSIDE

LUNE STREET

Preston
Station

BUTLER ST

FISHERGATE

Not to scale

212

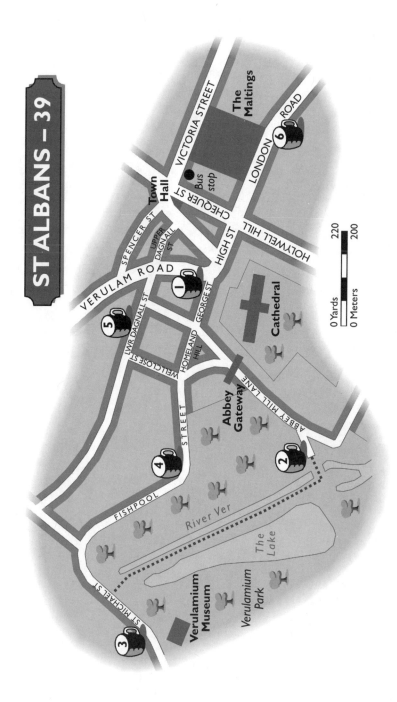

ST ALBANS – 39

Town Hall

Victoria Street

The Maltings

London Road

Chequer St

Bus stop

Spencer St

Upper Dagnall St

High St

Holwell Hill

Verulam Road

George St

Lwr Dagnall St

Wellclose St

Homeland Hill

Cathedral

Abbey Mill Lane

Abbey Gateway

Street

Fishpool

River Ver

The Lake

St Michael St

Verulamium Museum

Verulamium Park

0 Yards   220
0 Meters   200

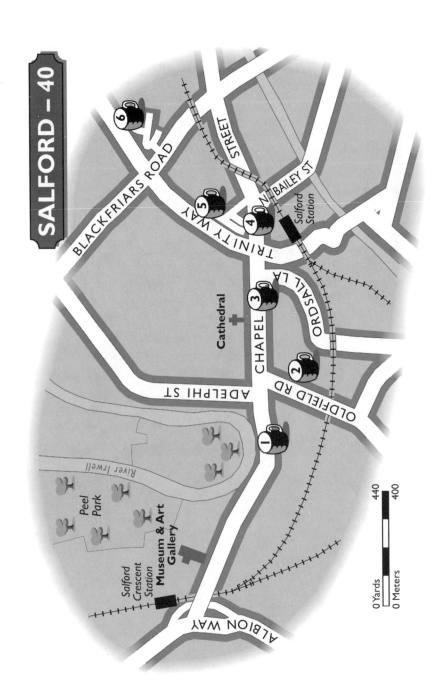

SALFORD –40

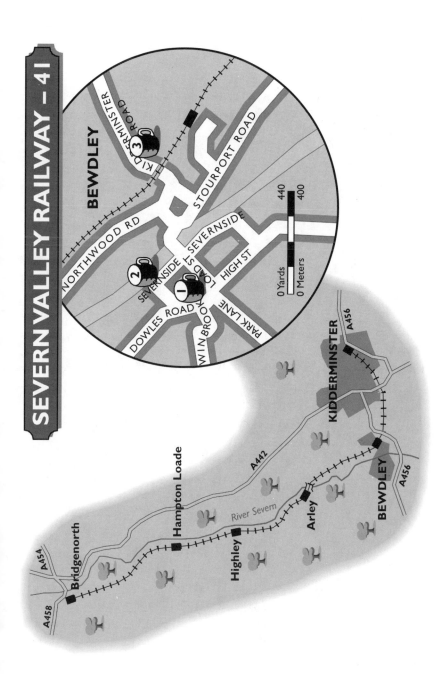

SEVERN VALLEY RAILWAY – 41

BEWDLEY

NORTHWOOD RD
KIDDERMINSTER ROAD
STOURPORT ROAD
SEVERNSIDE
SEVERNSIDE ST
LOAD
HIGH ST
DOWLES ROAD
WINBROOK
PARK LANE

0 Yards   440
0 Meters   400

Bridgenorth
A454
A458
Hampton Loade
A442
River Severn
Highley
Arley
KIDDERMINSTER
A456
BEWDLEY
A456

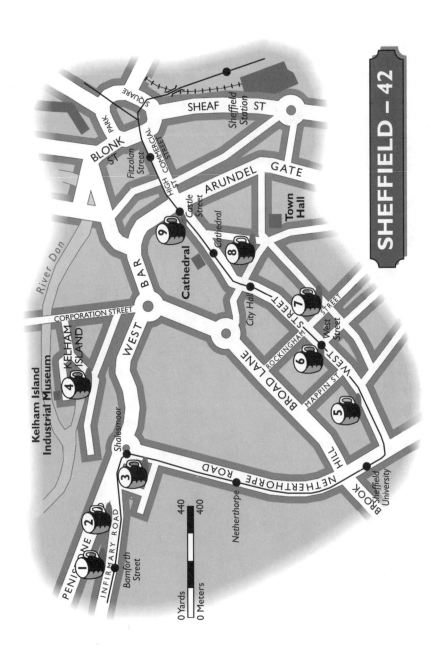

SHEFFIELD – 42

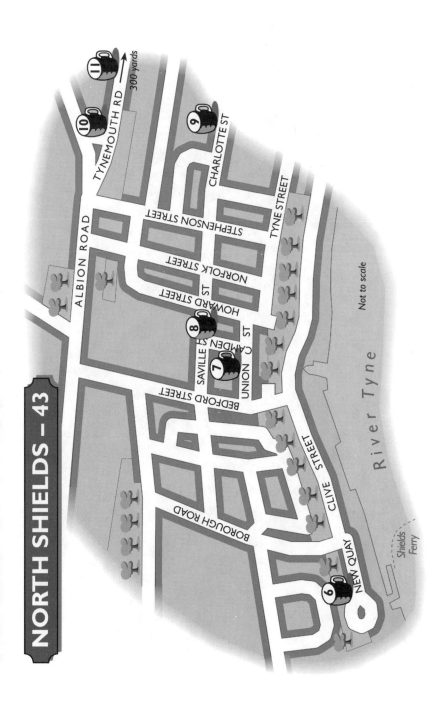

NORTH SHIELDS – 43

300 yards

River Tyne

Not to scale

Shields Ferry

ALBION ROAD

TYNEMOUTH RD

STEPHENSON STREET

NORFOLK STREET

HOWARD STREET

CHARLOTTE ST

TYNE STREET

SAVILLE ST

BEDFORD STREET

CAMDEN ST

UNION ST

CLIVE STREET

BOROUGH ROAD

NEW QUAY

6
7
8
9
10
11

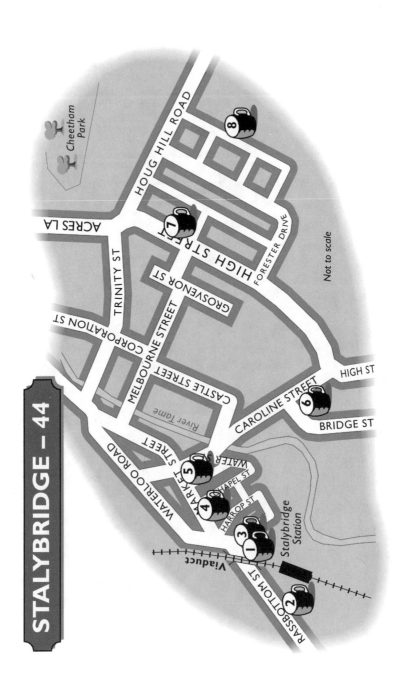

STALYBRIDGE – 44

Cheetham Park

HOUG HILL ROAD

ACRES LA

HIGH STREET

FORESTER DRIVE

Not to scale

TRINITY ST

GROSVENOR ST

CORPORATION ST

MELBOURNE STREET

CASTLE STREET

River Tame

CAROLINE STREET

HIGH ST

BRIDGE ST

WATERLOO ROAD

MARKET STREET

WATER ST

CHAPEL ST

HARROP ST

Stalybridge Station

Viaduct

RASSBOTTOM ST

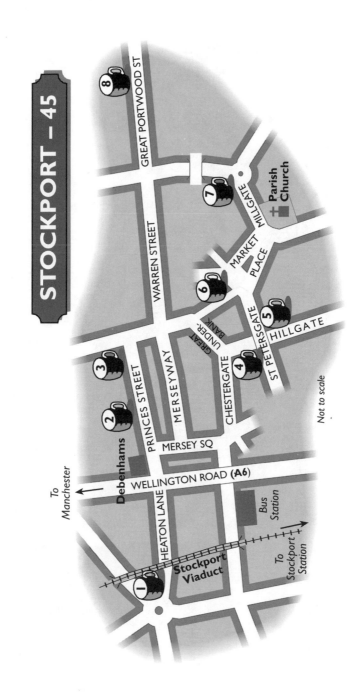

STOCKPORT – 45

GREAT PORTWOOD ST

8

MARKET MILLGATE

7

Parish Church

PLACE

WARREN STREET

6

GREAT UNDER-BANK

5

HILLGATE

ST PETERSGATE

3

4

CHESTERGATE

PRINCES STREET

MERSEYWAY

Not to scale

2

MERSEY SQ

Debenhams

To Manchester

WELLINGTON ROAD (A6)

HEATON LANE

Bus Station

To Stockport Station

Stockport Viaduct

1

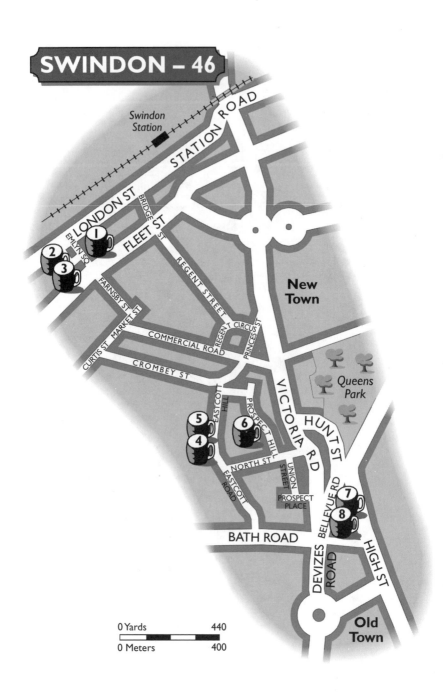

SWINDON – 46

Swindon Station

STATION ROAD

LONDON ST

EMLYN SQ

BRIDGE ST

FLEET ST

1

2

3

FARNSBY ST

REGENT STREET

CURTIS ST

MARKET ST

COMMERCIAL ROAD

REGENT CIRCUS

PRINCES ST

New Town

CROMBEY ST

EASTCOTT HILL

5

4

PROSPECT HILL

6

VICTORIA RD

HUNT ST

Queens Park

NORTH ST

UNION STREET

EASTCOTT ROAD

PROSPECT PLACE

BELLEVUE RD

7

8

BATH ROAD

DEVIZES ROAD

HIGH ST

Old Town

| 0 Yards | 440 |
| 0 Meters | 400 |

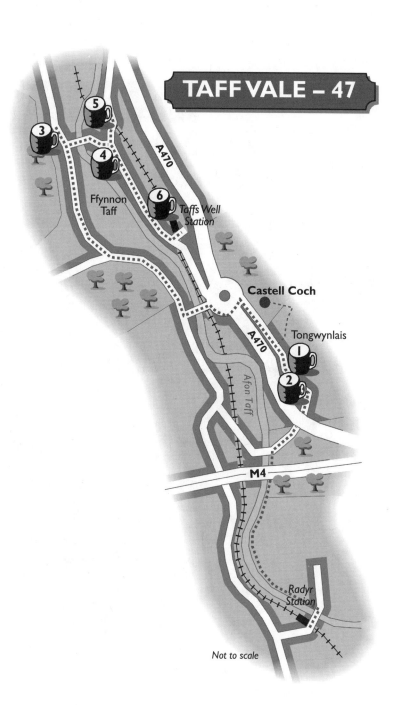

TAFF VALE – 47

3

5

4

6

Ffynnon
Taff

A470

Taffs Well
Station

Castell Coch

Tongwynlais

A470

1

2

Afon Taff

M4

Radyr
Station

Not to scale

WALSALL – 48

222

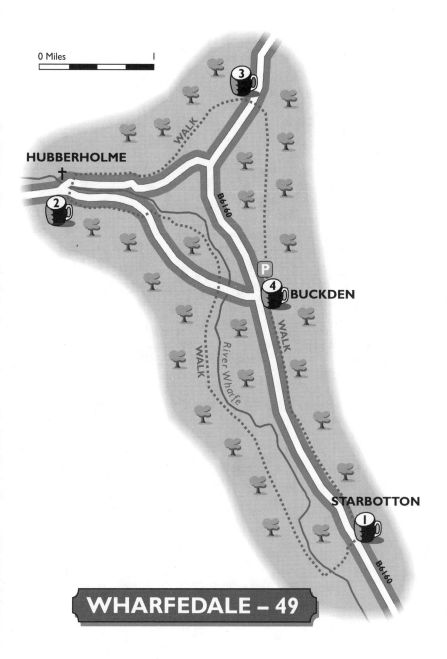

0 Miles | 1

③

HUBBERHOLME
✝

②

WALK

B6160

P

④ BUCKDEN

WALK

WALK

River Wharfe

WALK

STARBOTTON

①

B6160

WHARFEDALE – 49

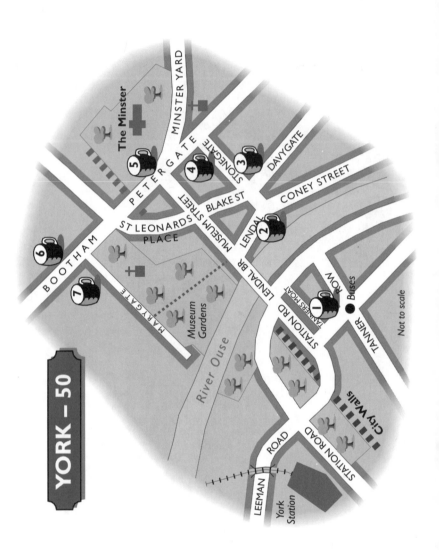

YORK – 50

The Minster

MINSTER YARD

PETERGATE

STONEGATE

DAVYGATE

5

4

3

CONEY STREET

BLAKE ST

ST LEONARDS PLACE

MUSEUM STREET

LENDAL

2

BOOTHAM

6

7

MARYGATE

LENDAL BR

STATION RD

TANNER'S MOAT

1

ROW

Buses

TANNER ROW

Not to scale

Museum Gardens

River Ouse

City Walls

STATION ROAD

LEEMAN ROAD

STATION ROAD

York Station

BEER INDEX

PUB INDEX *Page numbers in italics indicate photographs.*

230

OTHER STOREY TITLES YOU WILL ENJOY

The Good Beer Guide to Great Britain, a CAMRA/Storey book by CAMRA. This comprehensive guide rates the 5,000 best pubs throughout England, Scotland, Wales, and Northern Ireland. Includes full tasting notes on all British commercial beers. 560 pages. Paperback. ISBN 1-58017-101-X.

The Good Beer Guide to Belgium and Holland, a CAMRA/Storey book by Tim Webb. The ultimate beer lover's travel guide to the best cafés and bars of this beer rich region. Includes beer tasting notes on all local beers as well as maps and food recommendations. 228 pages. Paperback. ISBN 1-5807-103-6.

Brew Your Own British Real Ale, a CAMRA/Storey book by Graham Wheeler and Roger Protz. Features more than 100 homebrew recipes for recreations of well-known beers from brewers such as Bass, Fuller's, Guinness, and many more. Many of the recipes were created with the help of the brewers themselves and reveal some long-guarded secret ingredients. 196 pages. Paperback. ISBN 1-58017-102-8.

The Beer-Taster's Log: A World Guide to More Than 6,000 Beers, by James D. Robertson. This is the most complete reference available on domestic and international beers, with reviews of more than 6,000 beers. Entries for each beer include ratings on aroma, balance, visual appearance, flavor, and more. Other features include brewery names and locations from all over the world, an introduction to beer styles, and extra space for your own note-taking. 624 pages. Paperback. ISBN 0-88266-939-7.

These books and other Storey Books are available at your bookstore, farm store, garden center, or directly from Storey Books, Schoolhouse Road, Pownal, Vermont 05261, or by calling 1-800-441-5700. Or visit our Web site at www.storeybooks.com.